Mastering
LEADERSHIP

In the Christian Camp
and Related Ministries

How to be a successful camp leader

For counselors and those who have graduated to other key
leadership roles in the Lord's work.

By
David Burrow

McElroy Publishing
27-33 Fredonia Street * P.O. Box 488
Shirley, MA   01464

508-425-4055
800-225-0682

ISBN 0-9622191-6-9

ACKNOWLEDGMENTS

Only in eternity will I fully know why an Almighty God should choose me to write books for Christian camping. I readily yield to the many others in Christian camping who are more qualified than I. God has richly blessed me with inspiration for this book, with a capable artist who loves the Lord (Lynda Slattery), and with a publisher (Jack McElroy) who gives great interest and personal attention to getting this into the hands of those who can use it best.

This book is dedicated to my wife, Carol, who has been a loyal partner for over 30 years. She has mastered leadership in the finest and holiest sense and is a shining example for young women to follow.

TABLE OF CONTENTS

INTRODUCTION 1

1. A PERSONAL LETTER TO THE COUNSELORS . 5

QUESTIONS TO PONDER 7

2. LEADERSHIP -- WHAT IS IT? 9

QUALIFICATIONS FOR SPIRITUAL LEADERSHIP . 11

3. 10 THINGS EVERY GODLY LEADER MUST BE . 13

    Be a chosen instrument. 13

    Be willing to suffer. 14

    Be a servant. 15

    Be self-disciplined. 17

    Be a visionary. 21

    Be a seeker of wisdom. 22

    Be humble. 23

    Be filled with the Holy Spirit. 24

    Be willing to pay the price. 28

    Be a failure! 30

QUESTIONS TO PONDER 33

4. 20 POINT BIBLICAL CHECKLIST FOR
    LEADERS 35

5. 4 POSITIVE ATTITUDES 37

    Genuine Love 37

    Genuine Respect 38

    Genuine Communication 40

    Genuine Prayer 41

6. SPIRITUAL LEADERSHIP AND SPIRITUAL
    GIFTS 43

7. LEADERSHIP STYLES 47

8. LEADERSHIP QUALITIES TEST 51

QUESTIONS TO PONDER 54

TECHNIQUES OF LEADERSHIP 56

9. 5 COMMON MISTAKES TO AVOID 57

    #1 Accepting wrong advice 57

    #2 Failing to take the risk 58

    #3 Getting sidetracked 59

    8 Ways to Keep the Fire in Your Ministry.................. 60
    (How to Stay Focused)

    #4 Not acting the part of a leader. 62

    #5 Accepting the wrong job 63

10. 3 APPROACHES TO LEADERSHIP 65

    Direct 65

    Semidirect 66

    Nondirective 68

QUESTIONS TO PONDER 75

11. HOW TO MOTIVATE OTHERS. 77

WHAT IS MOTIVATION? 77

    I. Put campers together who will motivate each other. .. 78

    II. This is the way we do it here. 78

    III. Establish high standards of excellence. 79

    IV. Use group cooperation and enthusiasm. 80

    V. Expect the best from every follower. 82

    VI. Learn what they want; show them they can get it. . 83

VII. Break into a new area of learning. 85

VIII. Use failure as a motivator. 85

IX.   Build success upon success. 87

X.   Recognize the successes that are made. 88

XI.   Tell good success stories. 89

XII. Rewards. 90

      PRAISE AS A REWARD. 91

XIII. Use competition as a motivator. 91

XIV. Esprit De Corps is motivating. 92

XV.   How to overcome the destroyers of motivation . . . 94

      Conflict 94

      "There is only me." 94

      The complainer. 95

      Destructive criticism. 95

      Too much talk. 96

12.   HOW TO STAY ORGANIZED 99

13.   HOW TO EXPLAIN THE PC RULE WITHOUT
      CAUSING REBELLION 107

QUESTIONS TO PONDER 111

HOW TO BE IN CONTROL OF THE GROUP YOU
ARE LEADING. 112

14.   HOW TO LEAD IN FRONT OF A GROUP 113

I. Be prepared. 113

II. Relax and enjoy it. 114

III. Use good platform manners. 116

IV. How to handle the 5 MAJOR distractions. 117

15. HOW TO LEAD SONGS **123**

QUESTIONS TO PONDER **126**

16. HOW TO LEAD GAMES THE EASY WAY **129**

HOW TO DIVIDE THE PARTICIPANTS INTO
TEAMS: 129

WHAT TO DO WHEN IT IS YOUR TURN TO LEAD
GAMES 130

HOW TO TEACH A NEW GAME OR ACTIVITY 131

HOW TO PLAN A GAME TIME 133

CHARACTER TRAITS of AGES 6 TO 18. .... **135**

How to really understand others. 137

17. AGES 6 TO 11 .... **139**

18. AGES 11 to 14 .... **141**

19. AGES 14 to 18 .... **145**

20. BIRTH ORDER SEQUENCE" **149**

FIRST BORN CHILDREN 149

SECOND BORN CHILDREN 152

LAST BORN CHILDREN 153

QUESTIONS TO PONDER **155**

21. HOW DO PEOPLE LEARN **157**

QUESTIONS TO PONDER **161**

APPENDIX **163**

A. HOW TO PLAN A FULL CAMP PROGRAM. **164**
B. HOW TO LEAD A DISCUSSION **167**

INTRODUCTION

```
+-----------------------------------+
|  +-----------------------------+  |
|  |                             |  |
|  |          STOP               |  |
|  |                             |  |
|  +-----------------------------+  |
+-----------------------------------+
```

HOW TO GET MORE OUT OF THIS BOOK

Just take an extra minute to read this introduction to find out what this book is all about. It just might save you some frustration and save me some unjust criticism.

I write books for Christian camps, but this particular book has a much wider application. Since Christian youth resident camping is "my thing," that is the perspective of the book and that is where the applications are based. But since you are a leader, use your creativity to apply the many principles, rules and methods in this volume to your situation. Camp is only one application. Many times in this book you can take the word "camp" out and replace it with your own ministry: youth group, choir, Christian school, Pastor, Vacation Bible School.

WHERE ARE WE GOING?

The objective of this book is to help you use all the experiences and academic knowledge that you have thus far gained (use all that as the basic foundation) and then give you the challenge as well the specific steps to move UP to advanced and skillful leadership.

There are lots of young men and women in leadership positions, but very few have gained the skill that is needed to use those positions for the glory of God and advancement of His kingdom. Too often, young leaders only mimic what they have seen, or think they have found all the answers and so stop growing, or stumble along doing the best they can. Some even settle back into an attitude of pride and think their new leadership role is one of telling others what to do so they can do less.

TAKE THE CHALLENGE -- MOVE UP!

This book was designed to invite you to move UP from where you are now. There are many more challenges that you ought to tackle. Very few young leaders understand and apply the material that you will find in this book. This shortcoming makes them mediocre or even bad leaders. I am challenging you to be exceptional, to be the best, to be all that God really wants you to be.

GET READY -- GOD IS LOOKING FOR YOU!

God is constantly looking for men and women who can "fill the gap" by performing the needed ministry in the Lord's work. I want you to be ready when God is looking for the next person to be His leader. Leadership Principle #1 is quite alive and working in the world today. Let God's eye rest upon you.

YOU ARE IN A WAR.

Each time you move up the ladder in an organization (take more responsibility, gain a new title, have more power, experience more authority), you will be on a different battle field with Satan himself as your opponent. God want's your success for His glory.

2

Satan wants your defeat and failure for his program. If you do not know your opponent, you may be an easy target for Satan's deceptions and tricks. The higher up you go in leadership, the more subtly Satan undermines your ministry through you.

NUTS AND BOLTS -- HOW TO DO IT RIGHT

The second half of the manual is to expand your abilities in leadership. *How To Be A Successful Camp Counselor* gives all the basics in leadership; now it's time to expand on those basics and learn more insider secrets on being a leader of people (big people or little people).

When you reach the point where you think you know it all, you have begun to lose it. In spiritual leadership we are either moving forward or backward. The great spiritual battle will not allow us to stand still. If you want to be the man of God or woman of God that is totally available to God, then take this manual seriously and prayerfully. In so doing you will soon become an exceptional leader.

If you are NOT in a Christian camp context, skip the letter to the counselor that follows. See, I saved you time already! Thanks for not skipping the Introduction. A good leader can follow directions!

May God's richest blessings be upon you as you learn to yield yourself to Him.

♦ Special note: "the manual" refers to the book *How To Be a Successful Camp Counselor*. This is the basic text in learning to be a Godly counselor that fulfills the awesome responsibility of caring for children and youth.

1 A Letter to Second and Third Year Counselors

(To counselors, life guards, program director, game leaders, unit leaders, music director, cooks and other returning staff)

Dear Counselor,
Welcome back! Or should I say, "Welcome home!"

Isn't it great to be back with some of the friends you got to know and love last year? You are talking about all the things that happened over the school year, and of course, you share memories of last summer -- the funny things, "that" camper, the campfire meetings, that special night in cabin devotions, ... ah, memories! That's part of the reason you are back in camp. You have great memories of what happened, and naturally you are anticipating another summer like last summer.

THIS TIME you are not "the new kid on the block." You know your way around camp. You know the procedures, the rules, the traditions, the leadership. Maybe you have even moved up a peg from counselor to Head Counselor or even Program Director. There can be no question that you are part of the "in" group.

So who needs counselor training? Not you! You have this thing down pat. In fact, you might even be asked to help teach some of the sessions or be a group leader.

Assuming you have learned the techniques of handling a cabin full of children, and assuming you have the operations and ways of camp under control, what problems do you see ahead? How could another book on camp leadership be of any help? Where are the challenges for this summer?

How tragic it would be to just float through this season and only do what you are supposed to do. The Lord called this kind of person "an unworthy servant." The Lord expects us to stretch ourselves and be ALL that we can be. He expects us to go beyond the basic expectations of the job description.

For you, the camp and program can become routine. But for every camper, it is the highlight of the summer. These campers DO notice when you put yourself out for them. They DO notice your tone of voice. They DO notice that edge of real interest or boredom. And they very much want and notice your attention. This is true for those coming in the 5th and 6th week as well as those in the first week. Will you be the leader that these youth need? For more on how to actually accomplish this, see #3 of Common Mistakes chapter.

Do not miss the opportunities that the Lord is going to bring your way. As you give it all you have, so the Lord will give you blessings and other fringe benefits that you do not expect. In serving the Lord in camp, it is true: you cannot outgive the Lord when you do it all for Him.

For the campers,

David Burrow

David Burrow

MAKING IT LIVE IN MY SITUATION --
QUESTIONS TO PONDER

(From the Letter to Counselors and Introduction)

- In what ways can pride become a problem for second and third year staff or counselors?

- You face an enemy this summer that is far wiser, far more intelligent, and much more powerful than you. How do you plan to win when this enemy wages war in your ministry? What is your game plan?

- Do a self-evaluation of your abilities as a leader. Where are you lacking? How do you need to grow and to improve during this tenure of ministry?

- What are some positive steps you will take to not only keep old friends but to actively seek new friends among your peers?

- Can you think of campers that you had last year that left camp about the same as they came? What will you do differently this year to avoid that happening?

- How will you keep your focus on the campers instead of your personal discomforts, friendship problems, frustrations with camp, or problems back home?

- Do you remember last year how you began to run out of energy or patience or enthusiasm about the third or fourth week of camp? How do you plan to give the LAST week's campers and every week's campers your best instead of your left-overs?

7

♦ List the things that you remember about the BEST counselors (or staff) in camp last year. What are the things that made them outstanding counselors or leaders? After making this list, put a star by those items that you would like to work on developing this summer in your own life.

8

2   Leadership -- What is it?

Most people think of leadership as the guy up front who tells everyone else what to do. Sounds like fun. We all like to be in the place where we give orders instead of taking them.

Leadership has it's perks too: higher salary, special privileges, honor, power. These things are often attached to leadership because this person has worked his way to the top with education and experience. Many in the corporate world believe they <u>deserve</u> the promotion to leadership because it has been earned.

But can we in the Lord's work adopt these views and values? Is this really leadership?

Leadership is the ability to influence others to follow your lead. Having a title (like Counselor) can make those under your care do what you say, but that is not leadership.

As our Lord often did with other subjects, he took the subject of leadership and turned it inside out from what the disciples anticipated.

Spiritual leadership is having Holy Spirit power and influence working through you to guide others to yield to Holy Spirit control. This definition leaves out age, education, or even experience.

If you would be a spiritual leader, then you must be ahead of the others in your walk with Jesus Christ (your spiritual maturity). You are a true leader only to the extent that you <u>inspire</u> others to follow you as you follow the Lord.

The 10 Principles of Spiritual Leadership take us into the Holy place where God dwells, and we are again taught by the Master who is the original creator and designer of leadership. As you study these 10 principles, you will understand why some men with titles really do <u>not</u> have leadership, and others with no titles have tremendous influence. The challenge is for you to develop these into your life style, and then let the Lord give you the titles and positions when He chooses.

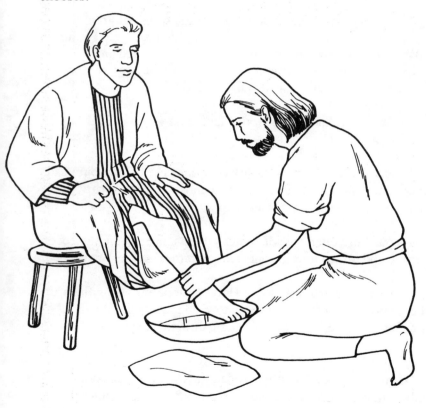

Qualifications

for

Spiritual

Leadership

3   10 Things Every Godly Leader Must Be

| PRINCIPLE #1 | Those in leadership in the Lord's

work are **chosen instruments** of the Lord.

Jesus said: "You have not chosen me, but I have chosen you." John 15:16

You cannot educate your way to the top or experience your way to the top. The only way to be a leader in the Lord's army is to be chosen by the Lord. In the following pages, we will discuss the qualifications of those that are chosen. But note this now: there are no shortcuts. Mere human qualifications just do not cut it.

It is exciting to realize that so few qualify that God is actually in a constant search for those that do meet His criteria. So if you can become qualified, you are almost certain of being chosen!

"The Lord has sought out for himself a man after his own heart." I Sam. 13:14

"I searched for a man to stand in the gap." Ez. 22:30

The best spiritual leaders are those that did not look for the job. God searched for a man (or woman) with the character and godly qualities needed, appointed that man, and then enabled that man. To be the person that God will choose, you must be the person of purity and character and godliness that meets God's criteria for leadership. Personal purity leads to public promotion because God

13

Himself is the One who sets up and takes down leaders. Many times the person God chooses did not ask for the job, much less aim to have it.

Yes, we ought to set goals. We ought to aim high. But the goals we aim to achieve are not goals of position or power or praise. Aim for the goal of Godliness. Or, as Jesus put it, "Seek ye FIRST the Kingdom of God, and all these things shall be added unto you." Seek for the Lordship and reign of Jesus Christ in your life, then let your Lord choose where you will serve, what you will do, and how high you will climb.

Your God given humility may be telling you, "God would never choose me. I don't have the abilities that so many others have." Do you think God would never choose you? That is just what David thought! Check out I Cor. 1:27-28 and be ready when the Lord calls you.

PRINCIPLE #2 Those in leadership in the Lord's work must be **willing to suffer** for the sake of the goals that are set before them in doing the Lord's work.

One of the great hindrances in camp is the staff member that is there for self. This staffer wants the perks, the comforts, the first place, the easier job, and/or the spot light.

Did you come to camp to suffer? Probably not! You may not be real crazy about sleeping out in the rain, hiking into the sunset, or eating hamburger with a dose of sand at the cookout. But that's all part of camp! As a leader, you are prepared to turn these physical discomforts into a challenge or even fun!

Suffering in camp is experienced when you give all you've got to give, and then you give a little more because it is needed. You might call it suffering when your days are VERY long and the nights too short. Putting yourself aside for your campers and for other staff should be the normal order of the day, but it does sometimes get tiring.

"Others first" must be more than just a nice motto on the wall. It must be your life message.

The reason that you are more than willing to suffer in whatever ways it comes is because you see a vision of every boy and every girl being touched by the Holy Spirit through the Word of God , stirring music, and the message of your own life. YOU can be the vehicle that God uses, or you can be a roadblock. God is looking for vehicles.

"but suffer all things, lest we should hinder the gospel of Christ." I Cor. 9:12b.   Philippians 1:29 to 2:11 is a beautiful section of Scripture to make your own.

PRINCIPLE #3 God's chosen leader is a person who has learned to be **a servant**.

Mark 10:43-44 "Whosoever will be great among you, shall be your minister, but whosoever of you will be the chiefest, shall be servant of all. For even the Son of man came not to be ministered unto, but to minister."

As you look at the great leaders of the Old Testament, you find great servants. God described Moses as "my servant."

In Mark 10 the disciples were concerned about who would be first (take the key leadership role in the Lord's new kingdom.). The

15

Lord responded to this line of thinking by reversing their whole concept of leadership. Instead of a leader being a boss, he is a servant!

Think about it. Who serves the MOST people in your camp? Yes, the camp director! He is a servant to <u>everyone</u> in the camp. In order to carry that responsibility of serving, he is entrusted with authority. But authority is only a tool that is used to aid in serving others. It is NEVER for self-serving purposes.

Jesus expressed it this way: If you want to find your life, you have to lose it. Those who lose their life, find it. As you "lose yourself" in being a servant to others and in giving all of yourself to others, then you will find yourself being the leader of those same people.

Here are six specific ways to make yourself into a servant:

♦   1) Rather than pal around with your friends from last year, see that new counselor that needs your encouragement. See that lone camper that needs help in gaining friends.

♦   2) Instead of expecting special privileges, honor or power, **be giving** these to others.

♦   3) Instead of being concerned about doing only your share of the work, want to always do MORE than your peers. Rather than thinking "what <u>must</u> I do?", as a godly leader you are thinking, "How much can I do?"

♦   4) You want **loyalty** from those under you, but that only comes after you develop a genuine loyalty <u>towards</u> these same people. Ask God to help you develop an intense loyalty toward those to whom you are responsible. Your love, loyalty and

16

dedication will inspire others to follow you. Remember, real leadership is the influence you have on others.

- ◆   5) Keep your mind on your ministry, not on your own problems. The devil often uses home problems, personal problems, friendship problems, staff problems, and physical problems to get our focus of attention off the _real_ problem -- fighting the devil in this great spiritual warfare! To win the spiritual battle, to be an effective leader, to accomplish God's purposes for this ministry, you must win the battle in your own mind and "lose yourself" in a passion for the ministry the Lord has given you.

- ◆   6) Whoever is under your care (is your responsibility), those people are the ones you are to serve. If you will grab hold of this principle, it will totally change your outlook for working in camp this summer. Your eye will always be looking for those that have a need This means that your needs, your wants, your preferences, your comforts are secondary to the ones you are serving. Yes, you are the big cheese -- feeding everyone!

PRINCIPLE # 4   Those in leadership in the Lord's

work must have a high degree of **self-discipline.**

The words "disciple" and "discipline" come from the same root word. A disciple is one who has disciplined himself to follow another one who is in authority. For the Christian, this means being in subjection to the Lord and exercising the self-discipline to follow His way of life.

When you make a commitment to be dedicated to your ministry, this commitment will greatly help with your **determination.** Without determination, it will be so easy to flounder or just plain fall. The

17

spiritual warfare is won or lost on issues of seeming insignificance. The snack shack holds more attraction than the vegetables at supper time. Does the Spirit control your time, your habits and even your eating? Do you give in to these minor temptations? Yes, these "minor" areas ARE important! We must be faithful in the little things if we are to be counted worthy to handle the major issues and battles. (Luke 19:17) **Dedication** is an essential for leadership.

Living a life of self-discipline is not very glamorous, but it is a vital part of learning to be a leader that is available for God to use. If you are faithful in the little things, God can trust you with the bigger things. God proves (tests, builds) his leaders by giving them MANY little things to do. It is like muscle building: just a little strain day after day slowly builds muscle that can handle big loads.

How to master 9 key areas of self-discipline

♦　　1) In the daily **schedule** it is so-o easy for the second year counselor to feel "above" the need to attend those early morning staff meetings or prayer meetings. It is tempting to use your advanced position and status to be late or find other things to do during the evening service. Don't cave in to laziness! (For much more help on how a leader develops his/her schedule, check the Index under "Schedule.")

♦　　2) Many people need a push to get started on something that needs to be done (like get out bed!), but the self-disciplined leader is a **self-starter**. The very nature of leadership means that you are out there in front of others. You are first. <u>You</u> have started the ball rolling. If your supervisor has to remind you to get going on something, that is a warning signal that your leadership is slipping.

♦　　3) Self-discipline will always be looking for and working on ways to **self-improve**. That is why you will be reading,

18

reviewing your training notes, asking questions, observing how others do it well, accepting suggestions (from peers, supervisors or campers) , and praying that God will reveal your weak areas and help you overcome them.

◆   4) **Self-control** of your emotions is an essential. Some folks easily "fly off the handle" or "lose their cool." A godly leader cannot afford that. Just ONE burst of temper can lose the respect of others. There can be NO exceptions. Remember, "there is no temptation taken you ..... but God will make a way of escape." I Cor. 10:13

◆   On the other extreme, neither can you be so **soft** that you are crying all the time. Working with people means that you will have compassion with those that are hurting. There are times to "weep with those that weep," (Rom. 12:15) and there are times to maintain your complete composure. You will need Holy Spirit self-control if you are a natural "softy."

◆   5) As you move up the leadership ladder, you will soon find yourself with responsibility for **handling money** or having authority to spend it. It is very easy to spend money that is not yours (just look at the government!). But you are responsible before God because the money you can spend is His money! Even if the money has been budgeted, use self-discipline to purchase only that which is needed, and get the best price, too.

◆   6) Real self-discipline comes into play when the first year staff take off for the week-end and you are stuck with the stay-over campers, or with the week-end clean-up jobs. When your supervisor asks you to do something, be the leader that is under self-control and submissive to God ordained authority, willingly and cheerfully **do exactly what is asked.**

19

* 7) It is hard, in the second year of counseling, to really **stay WITH the campers** as you ought. It is hard to be genuinely caring for EVERY camper. It is hard to be giving and giving and giving of yourself day after day and week after week. But being the disciple of the Lord and being called to challenge EVERY child to be like the Lord does require a high degree of self-discipline and self-sacrifice.

* 8) As you associate with your peer group in camp, you may find that they waste time or spend **time** in nonprofitable ways. You will experience peer pressure to do the same, but STOP! It is easy to lose that self-discipline when being casually swept along with others. The godly leader must think for himself:: "Is this the best use of my time? Is this what I should be doing now?" Yes, spend time with your peer group, but at the right time.

* 9) Many counselors each summer become ill because they did not exercise self-discipline in taking care of themselves. Too much sugar at the snack shack + too little nutritional food in the dining hall + too many late nights with the friends + a demanding schedule during the day = one sick counselor. A sick or run down counselor cannot give his best to the campers. Satan wins again! Taking care of yourself physically is another spiritual battle. Ask the Lord for the self-discipline to do what ought to be done rather than doing what feels good at the time.

    Those whom you expect to follow will be closely observing your own self-discipline. If they see a life in order, a life given for others, a life that is controlled by the Spirit, they will not mind when you ask of them that which is difficult or self-sacrificing because you have already set the example and standard.

20

| **PRINCIPLE # 5** |

Those in leadership in the Lord's work must be men and women of **vision.**

Can you envision the great all-compelling purpose of the camp ministry? Is that picture ever in your mind and driving you forward as the Lord's servant?

As you look at each boy and girl, can you see a man or woman who will have been moved by the Spirit of God during this week because you prayed and kept away the obstacles that interfere with His great desire for that life? Are you seeing a boy who will make a decision this week that will mold his life for centuries to come? Do you see a girl that can be committed to purity and thus saved from the ravages of sin in adult life? Yes, you may well have God's chosen instruments in your cabin for future teachers, pastors, missionaries and musicians. Will you do your part to mold this young life towards God's goals? Do you have a vision for each one?

Does your vision include what God may be doing in YOUR life? You will only be as effective and productive for God and His Kingdom as your own level of spiritual development. If you are to be a leader, you have to be ahead of those that are following. You are your own greatest obstacle to moving ahead for God. How might God want to use this camp experience to build you for some further work for Him? Is He laying foundation stones in your life upon which some noble building or work of God will stand?

Do you have a vision of eternity future? Does your imagination create pictures of that glorious heavenly home that Jesus has gone to prepare especially for you? All future rewards are built upon what is done here, on earth, this summer, in this camp. Your rewards in heaven will not depend upon your peers, but solely upon what you do for the Lord. You cannot give too much.

| PRINCIPLE #6 | Those in leadership in the Lord's

work must be those who **constantly seek wisdom**.

Col. 1:9 "....that ye might be filled with the knowledge of his will in all wisdom and spiritual understanding."

Prov. 1:7 "The fear of the Lord is the beginning of knowledge, but <u>fools despise wisdom</u> and instruction."

Wisdom starts at the bottom. A good leader must master (or at least know well) all the things that those under him are expected to do. To be at the top post in leadership means that you must experience all those tasks over which you will supervise others. For example, before I became a camp director, the Lord took me through the jobs of camp repairs, scrubbing bathrooms, cleaning cabins, mowing laws, washing dishes, cooking food, leading songs, planning games, teaching Bible class, preaching the evening messages, and being a counselor in a cabin for over 40 weeks. I even spent one day as the camp nurse! (That is like hiring an English teacher to supervise road construction!) As a camp director, I had walked in the shoes of those who I was supervising. It definitely paid off! By walking in those shoes I understood more of the frustrations, problems, joys, opportunities <u>and the importance</u> of each job (ministry!).

Chapter 1 of Proverbs is the story of wisdom crying unto men to come to her house and learn.

Wisdom will seek the help of supervisors when facing a new situation; pride will struggle through by oneself.

Wisdom will constantly read to learn more; foolishness will say, "I know enough. I need no more."

If you want to be a good leader you will not only seek to know and fully understand the tasks of those under you, you will be constantly learning the role of those over you. Do this by volunteering your help, by working alongside your supervisor, by reading , by asking questions, and by observing. Be ready if the Lord calls you to take the place of your boss.

Illustration: One Sunday I walked up the steps of this small country church where we were attending. The "old man" of the church met me at the door and said: "Well, I guess you're preaching today. They just took brother Gibbs to the hospital. He said he left his message on the pulpit."   There was no choice, I preached from his notes! It was only the grace of God that made it work out well in that emergency, but the Lord had been preparing me as I had been learning the role of the one over me.

As a leader in the Lord's work of Christian camping, there is SO much more to learn! Never stop seeking to expand your knowledge, abilities, and wisdom. Read, ask questions, observe how others do it right, and learn by putting it into practice. Learn from your leaders, from your peers, and from your campers!

| **PRINCIPLE #7** | Those in leadership in the Lord's |

work must have **humility.**

Read carefully and prayerfully Philippians 2:1-17. See our Lord's humility, Paul's humility, and the command for your humility.

Humility is a basic prerequisite for the Holy Spirit to use a life for the glory of God.

23

It is the Lord that lifts up one and puts down another. All true promotion in the Lord's work comes from the Lord. When the Lord needs a servant to take on more responsibility, the Lord lifts up the humble, not the proud. (James 4:6-10)

Pride turns people off (your campers and your peers), but humility draws people to you.

Pride will do all the talking; humility will do much listening.

Pride will not allow an honest self-evaluation, so others will be blamed for problems. This produces a staleness in one's personal growth and destroys the confidence of those that you would have following. Humility will accept correction in any form.

Humility will do any task that is asked or needed. Pride will look for the easy task, the notable task, or the clean task. We cannot choose where there will be a need. When that toilet is plugged by the previous user, do you look for the plunger or put up a note: "Out of order." Humility can be humiliating!

Humility will take responsibility for the goof, will ask forgiveness for the wrong, will stand by the one that is not popular, and will admit one's own weakness and inability.

Humility will accept the just and unjust criticism without counterattack or strong self-defense. Thank those that leveled the accusations and ask them to pray for you.

PRINCIPLE #8 Those in leadership in the Lord's work must be **Holy Spirit filled.**

In Acts 6:3 the preeminent qualification for even doing the most humble task was being filled with the Spirit.

"Be not drunk with wine, ... but be filled with the Spirit" the Bible says in Ephesians 5:18

HOW TO WIN THE BATTLE

In the Christian camp ministry there is a great spiritual warfare that never ends. Can you picture yourself, as a key leader, right in the middle of that battle? When Satan jabs you with one of his darts (temptations to anger, to revenge, to laziness, to apathy, to prayerlessness, to pride, to special privileges) your FIRST response is to meet that temptation on the human level (your own spirit). But to win that fight, you must meet the devil with the Bible and with the Holy Spirit in total control of you. You must see yourself in the Lord's army and on His mission field.

Were you chosen to serve at this camp because of your experience, your physical features, your education, your connection with the someone in authority, or your longevity at this camp? If so, maybe you should seriously consider resigning! THE qualification for your continuing ministry with children and youth is the Holy Spirit in control of your spirit. You need to be appointed by Him in order to qualify.

There can be only ONE controlling spirit if the camp is to be effective. If the Holy Spirit is pulling in one direction, and your spirit is pulling in another direction, not only will there be conflict, but the very purpose and heart of the ministry will be seriously thwarted. True unity in the camp is experienced when EVERY staff person is giving the Holy Spirit control of his/her life.

"Be filled with the Spirit" is in direct contrast to being filled with alcohol. When a person is drunk, they are under the control of the alcohol. When you are filled with the Spirit, you are under the control of the Spirit. You have yielded all control of yourself to Him.

ARE YOU CREATING THE SWEET SMELL OF THE SPIRIT IN THIS MINISTRY?

When a leader is filled with the Spirit, then he influences the new , young, immature staff member to do things the Spirit's way. As the spirit of the Spirit catches on, a very beautiful aroma fills the camp. Even casual visitors to the camp ground can "smell" the sweet aroma. Those who are not giving in to the Spirit either fade into a corner of quietness or else come under His conviction.

Unfortunately, this author has experienced very few camps where the Holy Spirit is given top priority in the lives of counselors, staff and administrators. The work of God is considerably thwarted because so many quench the fire which the Holy Spirit wants to bring.

The leadership role you play in camp is not so much dependent upon your official title as it is upon your walk with the Lord in walking in the Spirit. Remember, a leader is a leader because of his influence on others. You may be "just another counselor," but you may find yourself the unofficial "head counselor" if you let the Spirit direct your thoughts, actions, attitudes, decisions, and responses to others. Wherever Christians gather together, they can sense the ones that are controlled by the Spirit. I challenge you to BE that leader!

Even though you are responsible to the camp director and to the parents, you are primarily responsible to God. You can fulfill the required expectations of camp and parents and still fail as a godly influence in this camp. You have been commissioned by the Lord God Himself to watch over these children (and to fulfill other responsibilities).

26

5 STEPS TO BE FILLED WITH THE SPI.

To be filled with the Spirit simply means that you are letting the Holy Spirit take over your mind -- all your thinking processes. That is why every response to every situation will be controlled by God's Spirit in control of your spirit.

We need to be practical about how to be filled with the Spirit because it is critical to an effective ministry. Just how do you do this? How do you get filled with the Holy Spirit? Here are some very practical steps:

- ◆ 1) **Desire it**. The basic ingredient that seems so elusive is simply the desire to be filled with the spirit. That desire needs to be very strong. You have to really want it. The Bible often uses the term "seek." If you want to be filled with the Spirit, that means that you want to both be and do all that God desires. It means that you are ready to yield your will to His will.

- ◆ 2) **Renounce any known sin**. Pray from the heart: "Search me, O God, and know my heart. Try me and know my thoughts, and see if there be any wicked way in me." Ps. 139:23-24a When God reveals to you ANYTHING that is wrong, anything that is out of character with the Lord Jesus Christ, take care of it . Do what is right at any cost. The Holy Spirit cannot fill you and control you as long as you hold onto even small sins that you know about.

- ◆ 3) **Spend time with the Lord**. Give time with the Lord a top priority. Sometimes in the camp ministry you may have a staff meeting at 6:30 a.m. or be needed in the kitchen or at the pool by that hour. You just barely drag out of bed to make the schedule, much less get up earlier for meaningful devotions. The time of day is not as critical as the consistency. Take rest hour, take your time- off hour, take those 20 minutes before

27

supper or before the evening service. Take time when you are awake and alert and free from distractions. Go hide some place. But go!

◆ **4) ASK and keep on asking.** (Matt. 7:7) Remember when you were little and you asked your parents for something and did not get it? When you really wanted it (assuming it was something good), you kept on asking and asking. God is not offended when you show persistence in wanting His Spirit to take over your spirit. The problem is that so few people do it!

◆ **5) Practice the presence of God.** The proof of the Lord's presence is in your response to real life situations and relationships. As you meet each situation, use Scripture and pray your way through it. Don't even try to do anything on your own. Develop the habit of silent prayer as you are talking to others. Matt. 4:1-11

When filled with the Spirit, you will begin getting results that surprise you. Cabin devotions, Bible studies, personal counseling with campers, and other leadership times come alive with life and results. God is working through you. You are an instrument through which He is pleased to work. WOW! It's great!

"That's all there is to it?" Basically, that's it! In those basic steps you are yielding control to your Father.

PRINCIPLE #9 Those in leadership in the Lord's work willing to **pay the price** of leadership.

5 things it will cost you to pay the price of leadership.

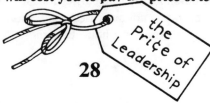

1. Jesus said that whoever would be first (the leader) must be last. Self-sacrifice is basic to leadership. As the leader, you don't count. The needs of others must always come first. This means you do NOT have a right to have a noisy cabin during rest hour or late at night. You do NOT have a right to any special food when eating with your campers. If there is a shortage of anything, you are the one to go without.

Paul the Apostle put it this way: "I have been crucified with Christ." Gal. 2:20 Crucified means that you are dead. "O.K. I'm dead. Who's watching the kids?" Answer: Christ in you. "Nevertheless I live, yet not I but Christ that liveth in me." We are calling this the price of leadership, but Jesus called it "the cost" of discipleship. A modern illustration is the picture of the throne of your life. Is the old Mr. Self sitting on that throne and ruling your life, or is Jesus Christ the King ruling your life? In the complex interrelationships and multiple leadership roles of camp, the answer to that question is not academic. The answer is seen by everyone around you. Ask them who they see in charge.

2. Loneliness is part of the cost of leadership. In the camp context, this means NOT taking time with your peers because your ministry is to your campers. As full and active and social as camp is, the leader can find himself starved for fellowship. That is why counselors and those in program often want to stay up late after the campers are in bed. This is not often wise. Accept the loneliness if your responsibilities require it. Serve your charges first! Remember, God sometimes keeps us away from others so that we will learn to draw upon His presence instead.

3. Camp is an exhausting ministry. Fatigue is part of the job description! Usually, any eternal work for God is achieved at the expense of someone's extensive outlay of energy. The leader who moves ahead of the rest is the one that puts more into the task at hand. This can mean longer hours, more study, thorough preparation, and

29

full effort into the implementation. Wisdom will then seek all the rest and recuperation that is available by wise use of time: rest when you can, eat all the fresh fruits and vegetables you can, and avoid all the sugars. A double dose of vitamins is almost a requirement to stay on top physically.

4. Criticism goes with the territory of leadership. The more you do, the more exposed your ministry becomes, the more people will have a "better" way to do it! As you rise in the ranks of leadership, know WHY you do <u>what</u> you do and why you do it the <u>way</u> you do it. Sometimes you will find unjust criticism from those that do not know your ministry or perhaps are jealous of your position or your expertise. Thank such people who confront you and ask them to pray for you. But do NOT let it get you down. If it is getting you down or taking the wind out of your sail, talk it over and pray it through with a supportive and caring friend.

5. Perplexity is part of mature Christian leadership. The more the Lord trusts you with responsibility, the less He will tell you what to do, directly. That is, He will leave the decision to your discernment rather than give you clear signs. However, as you lean upon Him, He will not allow you to make any major errors.

PRINCIPLE #10 Those in leadership in the Lord's

work must **be failures!** Don't be afraid to fail.

Have you experienced failure?
You were not in the cabin when the camper was injured. Unsupervised campers.
Cabin devotions just didn't fly. No one responded or participated.
You led songs, but the group was not cooperating or trying.
When in charge of staff devotions, the staff was sleeping!

30

The game you explained and conducted was a flop.

That counseling session with the problem person went no where.

You did your best, but the Supervisor thought you should have done much better.

On the cookout, it took over 40 minutes just to get the fire going.

If you have not yet experienced failure, you have failed because you are taking it too easy, not stretching yourself to your limit, or not volunteering for more difficult assignments.

Failure is a basic foundation stone for success.
In failure you learn that you have limitations.

Failure is a key ingredient to humility. You find that you are not the greatest. (The Lord cannot use a proud person. He sometimes sends failure to help mold a servant)

Failure helps you understand those under you who fail.

Failure drives you to ask for help, and thus becomes your best educator.

Failure makes you dependent upon God. You find your real strength and enabling in Him.

Failure is one of God's methods for making you the man or woman of God that He can use.

Failure is not the end of your service to the King; it is the beginning! Remember Peter!

MAKING IT LIVE IN MY SITUATION -- QUESTIONS TO PONDER

(The 10 Basic Principles of Spiritual Leadership)

Group Discussion:

Break the total group into smaller groups of three. Assign each group three Basic Principles and the following question. Regroup as a whole and share the conclusions.

" For each of the basic principles which are given, what would happen in this ministry if just <u>one</u> counselor or key leader did NOT follow that principle? What would be the implications and results? How would it affect his area of influence and the camp as a whole? "

Personal or group:

♦ What is leadership? What are the finest examples of leadership that you have experienced?

♦ As you look over the 10 basic principles:
Which ones got you excited about serving the Lord? Why?

Which one was new to you and made you think?

Which ones have you been living? How?

When you look back over your previous experiences in camp, which principle did you find the hardest to live out ?

Which ones did you clearly violate in last summer's ministry? What were the results?

♦ What is your vision for this summer's ministry? What do you want the Lord to do?

♦ How do you explain being "filled with the Holy Spirit?" What Scripture would you use to substantiate your view?

♦ What "price" did you pay to serve here last summer? What do you anticipate this summer? How will you handle it?

♦ List the times last year that you think you failed. Did they turn into a growing experience? Will you be building on those experiences this summer?

4   20 Point Biblical Checklist for Spiritual Leadership

Even though the following Scriptures were used to define the qualifications of the highest officers in the church, when you step into the role of spiritual leader (camp counselor, Program Director, recreation director, speaker, Bible teacher, or craft leader.), the qualifications are certainly no less stringent. In fact, in working with children and youth, the qualifications are all the higher because these young ones are so quickly influenced by your character.

Take the following list and check off those areas where you feel you have attained some degree of maturity. Then go back to those items that are lacking in your life, and ask God's help to add these things to your character. It may be best to ask for only one a week or even one a month. It's better to firmly attain one more strong area, than to have only a small sampling of everything.

From **Acts 6:3**

_____Honest report (good reputation)

_____Full of the Holy Spirit

From **I Timothy 3:2-6**

_____Blameless (above reproach or question)

_____Vigilant

_____Hospitable (make those campers feel welcome)

_____Apt to teach

____Not a fighter (argumentative)

____Not after money

____Patient (when everything goes wrong)

____Not covetous

____Not a beginner in spiritual things

____Humble

From **I Peter 5:1-7**

____Feed the flock - give them the Word of God.

____Serve willingly

____Do not "lord it over" your charges.

____Be a living example of Christianity.

____Submit to those over you, graciously.

____Serve one another.

____Don't worry. Give it over to God.

____Be on the alert for the Devil's attacks.

5   4 Positive Attitudes for Leaders of Youth

These attitudes are essential when dealing with youth (teens or children), but a wise leader will make the appropriate application if he/she finds himself as a leader of adults. The principles do not change with the age, but the exact application needs to be adjusted.

Genuine Love   A good leader will have a genuine love for the ones whom he is leading. There are two primary examples from whom we can learn.

The first example is the Lord Jesus Christ himself. Study how he expressed an active and genuine love toward his disciples. His was not a "put on" or something that had to be done because it was expected. Jesus really cared about those 12 guys. Sometimes he was tough, sometimes gentle. Examine his breaking heart at the Last Supper. Jesus was the supreme leader and our greatest teacher. Do you have Jesus' attitude towards those that you expect to follow you?

The second example is the dedicated Christian mother. See yourself as the parent of each of those over whom the Lord has given you responsibility. This is more true if you are the counselor in a cabin. Both the actual parents and even the campers expect you to play the role of a dedicated Christian parent. How does a parent love her child?

For specific ways to follow these ideal examples, study I Corinthians 13. The list given there is quite explicit about how one is to love another person.

As a leader you need the mental attitude of love towards your followers. That attitude will take care of most problems in your relationships because your followers and coworkers will see it in you. But if you want help in expressing that inward attitude in an outward way, think in terms of using your eyes, using appropriate physical contact, using discreet terminology, and using little actions of kindness that will get the message across.

How do you love an unlovely person? How do you have this positive attitude toward the repulsive, the obnoxious, the rude, the crude, the dirty, or the smelly one? Answer: God gives us problems so that we will find out that He has the answers. PRAY and ask God for a genuine love for the unlovely. The Holy Spirit delights to do a special work in our heart when we WANT to change and conform to the image of Christ. Also, pray for that person's needs (acceptance, confidence, trust in God, friendliness). If you really want to love the unlovable one, keep on asking (Matt. 7:7) God to give you a real love . He will!

As a leader you are a people builder. With the attitude of love, you will find it easier to encourage, to praise, and to look for the good and positive things in even the most repulsive.

Genuine respect Suppose you were home and the chief of police came to your house for dinner. Assuming this man was honorable and did an excellent job in your town, what would be your attitude while he dined with you ? How would you talk to him? Would you listen when he talked?

38

That is a picture of the respect that a good leader will have toward those under him. You would not be sarcastic. You would not be critical. If you disagreed, you would do so graciously and with all politeness.

You would respond this way because you would see your guest as either an equal or as one that was above you. In any case, you would give every courtesy.

As you think of those you are leading, think in terms of people (little people or big people) that are deserving of your respect. The Bible says that our mouth pours forth what is in our heart. It is therefore essential that we have a right <u>heart</u> attitude towards our followers. Consider two examples.

When there is a problem, a good CEO will call the employee into his office, sit him down, address him politely, and ask him questions about the problem or concern. Through questioning, he will gain an understanding of the employees viewpoint. He will respect that viewpoint, even if he has to correct the employee. The whole interchange is handled as one who is giving complete respect to another, and yet the leadership position is quite clear and mutually understood.

The second example comes from the extended family. Have you ever watched a skillful grandmother talk to her young grandson? She always makes him feel so grown up. She talks to him as an adult. By her smile and acceptance, and by her tone of voice and choice of words she wins the confidence because she conveys respect and caring. The child has the desire to live UP to the expectations, to live UP to the respect that is given.

A skillful leader will start with a mental attitude of genuine respect and then learn to convey that respect with tone of voice, manners, facial expression, volume, choice of words, attention given, and time dedicated to the follower.

Genuine Communication

The leader must be able to communicate with those that follow. He must be able to convey his thoughts, ideas, directions and so forth in a way that others will clearly understand. When working with children, this means that the words used must be understood. But more than that, clear communication must include tone of voice, the right inflection, facial expression, and even body language. It can include visual pictures, word pictures, or objects that help teach. If you are teaching, explaining rules, or inspiring those to follow you, then you must communicate what you want in such a way that the message is actually received.

However, a leader who does most of the talking, is not communicating. Genuine communication is a two way dialogue. You cannot lead if you do not understand what your followers are thinking. You may be saying one thing, but they are hearing something else. You may think your point is made, but they totally missed it. To really know what is being actually received or perceived by your followers, there must be feedback. They must communicate (send a message) back to you.

This feedback is sometimes picked up by facial expression. Questions from your group can give you a key as to just what they are thinking. But to be sure they are "on track" with you, ask questions. What you ask and how you ask depends on the particular situation. In a teaching context, you probably will use questions that relate to the context or to the response that you hoped to evoke. There are times when you will ask "feeling" questions: "How do you feel about ....?" "How did you feel when ......?" "How would you feel if .....?"

Based on the response from the questions, you will then structure and adjust your follow up communication or teaching or goals for the group.

A good leader will not do all the communicating. He will want to get regular feedback from his group.

Genuine Prayer For the Christian leader, prayer is not an "add on" or some ritual or obligation. It is a way of thinking that keeps him talking with the Heavenly Father about every boy or girl, about every decision, about every problem, about every task, and about every joy. "Pray without ceasing" is a command that a Christian leader needs to learn to live. When there is trouble of any kind, pray before, during, and after the problem.

The Christian leader has a very large advantage over the nonchristian leader. You can perform your responsibilities in the power of the Holy Spirit. You can actually experience God working through you! The key to have God's power in your life and ministry is to pray without ceasing.

When praying, use the most powerful prayers: Scripture verses. When you pray Scripture, you know you are praying in the will of God and have the mind of God. The scope of this book does not allow a deep study of prayer, so read the classic book *Prayer, Asking and Receiving* by John R. Rice, Sword of the Lord publishers.

41

6   Spiritual Leadership and Spiritual Gifts

● Which do you have?

The scope of this manual does not permit a full discussion of spiritual gifts. However, if one is to master leadership, he must have some understanding of how his own spiritual gift relates to his leadership style and ability. Since there is NOT universal agreement on the subject of spiritual gifts, the subject will be handled in a brief and cursory way.

The gift of organization or administration often makes a person a very strong leader. "Strong" in the sense of having a lot of drive, pushing ahead, being productive, trying new ways, and taking the lead. This is the person who has a vision of what can be done and thrives on organizing people to reach that goal. He makes decisions quickly and is decisive. If the Lord has blessed you with this gift, you need to be open to the Holy Spirit's teaching you through others.

♦   Being project oriented can make this person use others and not see the personal needs and feelings of others.
♦   A person with this gift needs to learn from those who have the gift of mercy and the gift of helps.
♦   If this gift is combined with the Choleric personality type, it is VERY easy for those under you to develop hard feelings because of your drive, rigidness, and high expectations.

The gift of prophecy is the second "strong" gift that takes considerable tempering by the Holy Spirit to avoid excesses. The gift of prophecy can see right through people and detect false motives or a bad spirit. The problems come when this person develops a critical outlook toward others. It is hard for this person to "step into the shoes" of another and feel with him.

- Handling those who have made mistakes or who have done what is wrong becomes a problem because of a lack of tact.
- It is too easy to dwell on the negative and jump to wrong conclusions.
- This person, too, needs to learn from the person with the gift of mercy. The need is to learn to speak the truth in love.
- If you have this gift, you will need to work hard on your relationships with others so that you can lead by your influence rather than by rebuke and criticism.

The gift of serving or gift of helps is the person who always wants to meet the needs of others. This person is quickly self-sacrificing in order to help others. He wants to do what needs to be done to relieve a problem as quickly as possible.

- As a leader, this person has a hard time delegating because he wants to do it all himself.
- The use of time is a problem. It may be frustrating to have so much to do, but once the hand is put to a task, there is not much concern for what is not being done. There is not a realistic comprehension of one's own limitations, so it's easy to lose track of time or get involved in things that are too much to handle.
- Saying "no" to someone who needs help doing something goes against the grain.
- If you have this gift, work on time management and priorities. Learn from the person who has the gift of organization.

The gift of mercy person is an extremely people oriented person. This one is sensitive to the heart needs of others. Usually this person is a good listener and has the ability to develop excellent counseling skills. Praying with and for others is a strong point.

- As a leader, this person has a hard time with delegating, with taking a risk (trying a new activity or doing something different), and in becoming a strong leader.
- It is hard for this person to be firm. The desire to be close to others and to develop relationships can interfere with the need to correct errors or give strong guidance.
- Being feeling oriented makes it too easy to hold onto offenses or be hurt by another's rejection. A good leader cannot afford to fall into these traps.
- This person needs to learn from the gift of prophecy and the gift of administration. There are times when one must have a "crust" to continue in the leadership role.

Whatever your spiritual gift, you want to use the strong points of that gift to enhance your leadership, and you want to learn from the strong points of the other's gifts in order to maintain a balance in yours. Our Lord Jesus Christ had the perfect balance between all the gifts. Learn from the best!

No matter what your gift, beware of the pitfall of expecting others to act like you and think like you. Others do not have your gift so will not have your strong points and outlook.

45

46

7   Leadership Styles

All that is said about leadership must be adjusted to the particular style of each leader. The style of each leader is heavily influenced by his personality type. Depending on which book you read, there are from two to eight or more personality types. Let's consider four basic leadership styles. This is important to understand because your leadership style will most probably be quite different from your supervisor or boss. If you have a friend who is also a leader, that person's leadership style will differ from yours, too. Even though we ought to learn from each other, it would be a serious error to try to mold your own style after another's. God made each of us unique, and we are most effective when we accept that uniqueness and develop it.

1. The Strong and Aggressive Leader.

This type of person is goal oriented, has a job to get done, sees the overall picture of what needs to be done, and pushes ahead to organize the task. Delegating comes naturally, as does decision making. All people and things can be seen as resources to get the task completed. Unless tempered by the Holy Spirit, this person can run right over others and not be sensitive to others' needs and feelings. This is the "take charge" person who often rises to the top of organizations.

2. The Peacekeeper.

This type of person does not like conflict, is easy going, rarely gets upset over anything (great in an emergency!), and tries to keep everyone happy. This person does research to check things out. He/she may be good at detail or planning, but may not be as aggressive as needed in a leadership role. This leadership style is much softer and easier going than the Strong Leader. People often like this person and get along well with him.

3. The Socialite.

This person loves people. Whenever you talk to this person, you get the distinct feeling that you are very important, until the next person comes along. As a leader, this person has a very hard time with detail, planning ahead, delegating, maintaining a neat environment, and organizing. Although individual Socialites often gain some of these skills. This person is very strong on caring about others ,being sensitive to their needs, and often has creative ideas and some artistic touch in some way.

4. The Artist.

This person is often strong in some artistic area or music. He/she is good at details, sees things that need to be done, sees problems in what the Strong Leader overlooked, and has a very big heart for people. This person can learn to be a stronger leader, but telling others what to do and demanding that others follow does not come easy. In the peer group, this person may often back off from leadership roles.

Do you see yourself? Which one is your boss or supervisor? Can you see why there can be conflict between different leadership styles?

There is no "ideal" leadership style. All of them are good. Each one has strengths and weaknesses. As a leader, you need to identify yourself, see your weaknesses, learn from others, and utilize your strengths.

48

In working with others, you will find some that are very strong in one of the above categories. Be patient and understand why they do it the way they do. Many leaders you will see have some combination. The ideal leader will learn the best of each and avoid the pitfalls of all. That's Jesus!

8 Leadership Qualities Test

This list is a self inventory that ought to be reviewed when you think you are a fantastic leader and when you become impatient with those that you are leading. If you rate yourself over 90% on this list, have three of your peers or supervisors rate you (hint: you will NOT score near 90%!). The objective of this list is to help you maintain that level of humility that is needed in a good leader and to give you specific goals to choose for improvement in leadership. When a leader thinks he has "arrived," that attitude is the beginning of the end of his leadership. Put a check mark by each item that you need to work on.

_____ Are you SELF confident (instead of confident in God's ability, presence, power, and love)?

_____ Are you a student of men (learning behavior patterns) AND a student of God?

_____ Are you SELF ambitious (instead of burning with a desire to lift up others)?

_____ Do you enjoy telling others what to do, or do you enjoy obeying God and finding His will?

_____ Have you ever broken yourself of a bad habit? Self-discipline is a key to good leadership.

_____ Are you calm during a crises event and don't "lose it" when under pressure?

_____ Do you have a healthy independence so that you can make your own decisions, and yet you know when it's time to ask for help and counsel?

_____ Do you take criticism graciously and ask the Lord to reveal the truth in it?

_____ Do you use failure as a stepping stone to improvement or correction?

_____ Do you choose for friends those who improve your character?

_____ Do you win the cooperation and confidence of others?

_____ Do you have the trust and confidence of those in authority over you?

_____ Can you exercise discipline upon others WITHOUT using force?

_____ Can you move into a conflict situation and bring peace?

_____ Can you influence others to do some of the dirty work that is needed and lead them in doing it joyfully?

_____ Can you conduct your ministry of leadership without depending upon praise or approval of others?

_____ Are you at ease with your supervisors, your campers, and their parents?

_____ Can you quickly make those under your authority comfortable with your presence?

_____ Do you have real respect and love for the dirty little camper who doesn't take a bath and uses bad language?

_____ Are you a tactful person who can say the difficult thing in the right way?

_____ Are you quick to forgive and have a short memory of personal offenses?

_____ Are you optimistic? Are you mostly positive in thinking and attitude?

_____ Do you welcome responsibility and opportunity?

_____ How do you handle another person's failure that affects you? Graciously? Forgiving? Understanding?

_____ Do you see your responsibility as one of LIFTING UP those under you? Even if that means that they will pass you up in rank?

_____ Are you an encourager of those around you?

_____ Are you a listener? Or do you find yourself doing most of the talking?

_____ Are you enthusiastic? Can you get excited with your campers? Do you have LIFE?

MAKING IT LIVE IN MY SITUATION --
QUESTIONS TO PONDER
(Biblical Qualifications, 4 Positive Attitudes, Spiritual Gifts, Qualities)

Group Discussion:

Group together all those that feel they have the same spiritual gift. Make a separate group of those that have no idea, unless the group leader has other material or tests to help them discern where they fit. Have each group discuss these questions:

♦ How have we experienced in our ministry a conflict between our spiritual gift and effective leadership?

♦ How has our spiritual gift been a benefit?

♦ What are the strong points of our gift that we should be encouraging in others?

Group Discussion:

♦ Take each of the qualities for spiritual leadership. Describe one person that you know that exemplifies that quality. Choose a layman, not a pastor, missionary, or evangelist.

♦ Why do you think it was hard to think of someone? Should not the persons on both sides of you qualify?

♦ Without naming anyone or describing anyone, think of someone who is the opposite to each quality. What is your reaction toward that person?   How would you feel if that person where over you in a leadership role?

◆ When you think of a good leader, which of the things in the Leadership Qualities list naturally come to your mind? Why?

Personal:

◆ Go through all these check lists and actually do them. Put a mark by the ones that you feel you have fulfilled. Yes, you are still working on it, but at least it is not a major negative or a problem.

◆ Now go over these lists and study the ones that are blank. You do not feel strong in these areas. Very prayerfully talk this over with your Lord and ask Him: "Which ones do you want me to work on now?" It might be best to choose two or three rather than attempt too much at one time.

There is great value in knowing that you have not yet arrived. Part of humility is seeing that you have growing to do, but others have already arrived in certain characteristics. It is good to look up to others so that you are not tempted to look down on them.

If these lists revealed to you some real problem area over which you are not getting the victory, take the opportunity to talk to some real men of God or women of God in this ministry. Humility will ask for help.

Techniques

of

Leadership

9   5 Common Leadership Mistakes to Avoid

(Even the best leaders often trip on at least one of these!)

| MISTAKE #1 |
Listening to the wrong advice at the wrong time.

1. **Get all the facts when faced with a problem.** You are brought a report about something that is negative. Something happened or someone did something or said something that is not good. The person who brought you the report is somewhat upset and/or putting some pressure on you to do something about it SOON. STOP! Do nothing. Make no decision.

Your first move must be to investigate and get all the facts. If others are involved, get the other side of the story. If it is a physical problem (toilets are overflowing) , go check it out yourself. Do not make any decision until you have all the facts.

2. **Stick to your plans.** You have planned the game time or song time or evening service or cookout. You thought it all through. You know what you want to do and how you want to have it done. Then someone comes up (usually at the last minute) with "a better idea." This person has NOT done careful research or put careful thought into it. He just got an idea and thinks you should do it his way. STOP! Do not change your plan. Politely explain that you are doing it this way because, or that the plans are made and you feel it would be best to follow through with the plans.

3. **Don't let good ideas get killed.** You are excited about an idea. You share it with someone else. He gives you a blank look. Immediately he comes up with two or three reasons why it won't work. Sift through his advice in case there is something you are overlooking, but generally DON'T LISTEN! Others do not share your enthusiasm and have not been thinking about this for some time. This leads to mistake #2

MISTAKE #2 Failing to take the risk.

The very fact that you are a leader and have responsibility means that you must take risks. It is far easier to sit back and criticize a sermon than it is to write and deliver one. It is far easier to play a game than it is to plan and lead one. By being a leader, what you plan and what you direct has the possibility of failure or problems. That is risk. **Leaders who will not take the risks are not good leaders.**

Take the risk. Find some different songs to sing and teach them to the camp.

Take the risk. Plan a different "hide and seek" game. Try some new twists to it.

Take the risk. Rearrange the afternoon program if there are problems or just missed opportunities.

Take the risk: new ideas, new schedules, a new approach, new activities, new ....

Reduce the risk by doing your research, by planning carefully, by having full preparation, and by asking others for input (but avoid the "wet blankets" who specialize in putting out the fire).

MISTAKE #3	Getting sidetracked from your

real ministry.

Camp has many different facets: program, relationships, physical facilities, challenges, spiritual warfare, financial planning, purchasing, and lots of fun things to do. As you move up the ladder of leadership or as you spend more than one year in the same camp, it gets easier and easier to get sidetracked from your primary responsibility.

Keep in mind exactly why you were asked to serve in this ministry. Are you fulfilling that role? Are you doing the job? Are you improving?

Second and third year counselors often get sidetracked with "someone special," planning a part of the program, building something in camp, making something in the craft shop, or even helping in the kitchen. The problem is that these counselors are somewhat bored with the routine of the job and have lost sight of the children that need their love, attention, and counseling.

Boredom or routine can be a major sidetrack. Do you remember the time when Jesus was bored with helping people all the time? I don't remember that time either. You are probably in your ministry for the summer or forty to sixty hours a week. Jesus did a stint of 24 hours for three years! Why didn't he get tired of it all? Romans 8:6 is just one place where the cure for boredom or routine can be found.

"To be carnally minded is death (as in "bored to death.")"
"Carnal" means of the flesh, self, not spiritual, not Christ centered.

"But to be spiritually minded is *life* and peace." "Life" as in the opposite of boredom, being productive, not conscious of routine. If you want your ministry to be dynamite instead of wet gun powder, the next verses tell us that we need to stay focused on the things of the Spirit. So let's nail down just how we can do that, whether you are ministering to campers or to others:

8 WAYS TO KEEP THE FIRE IN YOUR MINISTRY
(HOW TO STAY FOCUSED)

1. Ask the Lord to help you **"pray without ceasing."** You can develop the habit of praying for those to whom you are responsible when you are with them, when you see them coming toward you, when you are waiting in line, when you are listening in chapel times, and when you lie down.

2. Some place in your hectic schedule, set aside some time just to **"be still and know that I am God."** Read the Bible for yourself (not in preparation for something coming up). Ask God to speak to you. Just slow down and give God a chance.

3. Whether you have a ministry to campers or to other counselors or staff, **set prayer goals** for each one. What do you want God to do in their lives while under your leadership? Write these down, and pray through this list at least twice a day. Write down when God answers, and be sure to share those joyous answers with others! Daily ask God to keep in front of you the needs of those under you and a vision of what they could become. This keeps your focus off yourself and on others, just like Jesus did.

4. As you start and then go through each day, talk over with the Lord just **what HE wants you to do** today. How are you to

60

minister to others? What goals have you set for yourself? What are the real priorities?

5. If you are having trouble staying on course (being focused on your real responsibility), ask another friend/coworker to keep an eye on you and **hold you accountable**. Every day or two, ask each other, "How am I doing?" Be honest with each other, be mutually supportive, and pray together.

6. At least once a week, go through those checklists of "Qualifications for Leadership." in this text. Choose one or two areas where you are weak or even failing. Set these as **goals to accomplish**, with God's constant help. Make them real prayer concerns. By **challenging yourself** this way, you will stay fresh and alert.

7. Fatigue can defeat you physically, and that leads to defeat spiritually and emotionally. So make yourself get that **extra rest** (you will <u>not</u> feel like you need it), stay away from the sweets, eat more protein, and eat all the fresh vegetables and fruit you can get. Double dose on natural multiple **vitamins,** too!

8. Be loyal to the ones for whom you are responsible. Do the job that you were employed to do. If the Lord wants you to move to a different facet of camp, let Him do the moving.

| **MISTAKE #4** | Not acting the part of a leader.

♦ **Your dress:** In our informal society, too often a leader "dresses down" more than is appropriate. In camp, it's fine to wear the crazy hat, the loud shirt, the purple shoes. But as a leader, never look "slummy." Always look neat, clean and sharp. Your dress can invite or reject the influence that you need in order to lead.

61

♦ **Your language** must be appropriate for a leader. Many young Christians are now using terms that were heard only in the city gutters a few years ago. Using questionable terminology will not gain respect or following. The wrong language can kill the ministry and create problems beyond our control. (see James 3) Use only the best in language. Jesus said: "Let your yes be yes and your no be no." (Matt. 5:37) Follow Jesus' advice; He was a great leader!

♦ **Your manners** ought to be the best. Not only do girls go first (or, for the female leaders, campers go first), but all manners ought to be above reproach or question. Be careful about "practical jokes," how you address your peers, how you behave at the table, and your conduct in chapel. As a leader, you want others to look UP to you. Develop the BEST in manners, no matter what your other peers may do. Be the leader that is available for God's promotion.

Take the leadership role that your followers expect you to take. You are not "one of the gang." You are in charge. For the balance in being the authority, see the following chapter on the three approaches to leadership (Direct, semidirect, nondirect).

| MISTAKE #5 | Being in the wrong place.

You may make an excellent counselor but a terrible program director.

You may be an excellent nurse, but a terrible cook.

Camp is great place to try out different jobs. As you have opportunity, take as many different jobs as you can. But when you find yourself in a place or position that just does not fit, ask for a transfer, promotion, or demotion.

Know your talents, and your limitations. Too often , man made promotions take a person who is excelling in a servant role and place him in a supervisory leadership role. Before you accept a promotion, are you moving into a place that God has prepared you to take? Does it fit your abilities and gifts?

Be a leader where you fit, not necessarily where someone is desperate for a hole to be filled. Know when to say, "Thank you, but no. "

When you **DO** understand what God has given you in a particular set of abilities and interests, then strive to be the best you can be in that area of ministry. As you master one level, ask for a promotion to the next level. Usually this takes two or three summers or years. Leaders have to take the initiative. Just be sensitive to God's timing and be willing to wait for the right time.

10   3 Approaches to Leadership

(How to use each one at the right time.)

When looking at the three approaches to leadership, there is not one right way. Each approach has a context in which it is best used. To become a skilled leader, you will want to become proficient in all three approaches and adjust your leadership to use the right approach at the right time.

DIRECT This is the one that comes to mind when most people think of leadership. You see the person in front of the group either teaching or directing in some way. **In the direct approach, the leader is telling the group exactly what is wanted or is giving directions on what to do.** The group is then expected to follow or respond in what the leader is asking them to do.

When to use it.

There is nothing wrong with this approach. Use it when you are in front of a group in a meeting such as a Bible study or evening service. This is the method that is usually used when explaining rules or explaining how to play a game. A counselor in camp will usually use this method to keep the campers on schedule and get them to the next activity. This is used in chapel to keep the camper's attention on the leader up front and to keep them quiet.

This is the method Jesus used when teaching on the mountain or at the seashore.

For specific help in how to use this approach, see the chapter on "How to Lead in Front of Group."

Your leadership effectiveness will expand if you do not stop at this approach. There are times when another approach will be much more effective in getting the response that you desire.

SEMIDIRECT You know where you want the group to go in their thinking or conclusions, but rather than just telling them, **with questions help the group come to those same conclusions.** This is not a game of "guess what I'm thinking of." The conclusions are not specific, but general. There is plenty of room for the group to come up with ideas that are new, then you as a leader need to evaluate the appropriateness of following through with some of these ideas.

When to use it.

If you are the counselor , rather than giving a list of rules the first night of camp, <u>after</u> giving a little pep talk about "this is going to be the BEST cabin group and we are going to have the GREATEST week of the summer," you would say something like this : "What do you think should be some of the rules of our cabin group so that we can accomplish this? What rules will make us the BEST and give us the best week?" When you continue to guide them with key questions, probably you will end up with about the same list of rules you had last week!

Another example would be the group dynamic technique called "brain storming." With this one, you ask the group for ideas or suggestions on a particular topic. The rules of this discussion is that any idea is acceptable. You are only going to make a list. If you are

66

working with other counselors or program people in planning for after-supper fun times, ask: "What are some options for activities?" Then write down all the ideas. Nothing is discussed and nothing is excluded. AFTER the list is complete (no more ideas are coming), then go to phase two: "Let's go through this list and see which ideas would best fit this next week in camp. Which ones do you think are workable and would give the most fun to the campers?" Rather than start from the top of the list, ask the group to choose the best from the total list. Then discuss the ones chosen and start working out the details.

When it works best.

The semidirect approach works well when you are planning a project or want to reach a goal such as putting together a camping trip, planning a project, working on a special event such as a banquet night, doing group evaluation, or conducting a problem solving session. You are drawing out from your group the details of how to do it and steps to take to reach your goal. You will find that within any group are ideas that never crossed your mind, but they are excellent ideas.

What it can do for you.

Using the semidirect approach will (1) open up a vast resource of information and ideas, (2) will draw the group together in a wonderful unity of purpose , (3) will help the group learn to work together, (4) will help the group value each other more, (4) and will demonstrate your personal confidence and appreciation of each member of the group.

Jesus often used this method when dealing with the Pharisees in the temple. He used it with the woman at the well. He used questions to take charge of the situation and have others follow him.

Nondirective

The leaders role in nondirective leadership is twofold: observation of individuals and group processes and the creation of questions. The leader uses questions to draw out the group's and the individual's understanding of (1) the group dynamics, (2) the part each individual is having in the group, (3) problems that need to be discussed, (4) and how the group needs to help certain individuals.

When to use it.

This approach is used in the context of a group working on a project or goal of some kind. The leader is the coordinator or facilitator (makes it happen). The goal or project may be planning an outing such as a canoe trip or backpacking trip. It may be the actually carrying out of such a trip: where to go, who sets up camp, what do we eat, who is doing the cooking, how do we get the fire started, when do we get up, ... The solutions to all questions are worked out by the group rather than directed by the leader. If the group is headed in a direction that will be in some way harmful or create a problem that is not productive in its working out, then the leader steps in with questions, suggestions or even direct leadership.

Why use it.

There are three primary reasons for using nondirective leadership: to get something done (accomplish a task), to learn about the dynamics of the group by learning about the individuals and how they react and relate, and to help the individuals in the group understand themselves and overcome weak points.

Of the three objectives, the first (getting the task done) is considered the least important. The accomplishment of the task is almost a byproduct of the last two objectives.

68

Even if you do not use this approach, the following material can be used with the semidirect approach to increase your own sensitivity to what is happening in the dynamics of a working group.

For the leader to be effective, he must have some understanding of what is happening in the group. Observation must be coupled with a mental (or literal) recording of what is happening. Here are some things that ought to be noted:

What to observe in a working group.

When there is any type of group discussion or verbal interaction:

- Which ones do most of the talking? Who rarely speaks?
- During the process of the project, have some become more quiet and others more vocal?
- How does the group handle those that are silent? Do some members try to include these people? Are they totally ignored by others? Is there an attempt by anyone to draw them in?
- Who seems to take over and give direction? Who does not want to follow? (note facial expressions)

As the group is either in discussion or moving through a project:

- Which members seem to have more influence on the group than others?
- Who is more respected? Who is just tolerated? Does everyone really listen when a particular person speaks?
- Is there any friction in the group? What are the causes? (It may go back to circumstances BEFORE this particular group came together). How do you plan to help these two work this out?

As the group either plans ahead in how to handle the project or is in the process of moving through the project, decisions are being made by the group. The leader should note how those decisions are made and who in the group influenced those decisions:

- Does one person force his will on the others?
- Is there thought about how the decision will affect each member of the group?
- Example: "We will hike 10 miles today and camp on top of the second mountain." Is there consideration for the older person? For the person who is not used to carrying a pack? For the person who has a hard time breathing in high altitudes?
- Who takes part in the decision making process with ideas, objections, or alternatives? Who does not take part?.
- Who is very positive or even enthusiastic about whatever the group seems to decide?
- Is there concern for the majority? Is it controlled by a vocal and strong minority? Do all the members participate in the decision?
- What happens when a suggestion is made and no one listens or responds? Does that individual try again? Quit? Join with the group? Silently rebel?

What the leader does.

The leader's role in this ongoing group decision making is to help the group become increasingly sensitive to each other and each other's needs. Things that the group is overlooking the leader will bring to the group's attention with a question. Example: "We've decided to hike for ten miles today. Who has had no input into this decision?" The group would then have to mentally go back over the discussion, look around the group, and take responsibility for overlooking certain members. When these quiet members are given an opportunity for input, the group decision may have to be reevaluated and perhaps changed.

As the leader becomes more sensitive to the group dynamic and who is doing what, there will emerge at least *four distinct individuals* within the group. Each has a definite contribution to make. A good decision will get input from each type of person:

◆ 1. **The Organizer** will be the natural leader who wants (1) production , (2) efficiency, and (3) organization. He will tend to be impatient with so much discussion. He is task oriented and wants to get moving ahead. He may tend to overlook people and not see the needs of others. But he will be a great help in organizing, delegating, and overseeing the whole project.

◆ 2. **The Feeler** will be very sensitive to others. This one is so people oriented that he is talking all the time, in a corner consoling someone, praying over another's needs, and angry at the Organizer for pushing so hard. If someone is hurting, this one will pick up the message. In a discussion, this person will be sensitive to the ones who are not participating and want them brought in.

◆ 3. **The Worker** is busy packing up, cleaning up, putting things in order, and probably helping others. He is quite happy to be told what needs to be done and will jump to meet that need. In discussion he may be more content to just "amen" whatever anybody wants to do.

◆ 4. **Mr. Detail** is very slow to move until all the facts are known. He can bog down a discussion with wanting to know all the details, but he can be a great help in uncovering areas to be considered that others overlooked. If you think you might be forgetting something, ask him. This one can slow things down because everything has to be done "just so."

How is the group functioning?

71

The nondirective leader is also looking for how the group is functioning. When the group is in any way hurting each other, the leader needs to step in with questions and give a new direction or new sensitivity:

- Does one person cut off another when speaking?
- Is each permitted to get his idea or input across?
- Do any group members seem to enjoy provoking others?
- Are most involved? Interested? Or bored?
- Are there subgroups that stick together? Do they have their own agenda? Do they pit themselves against the rest? Do they participate with the others?
- Are there issues that ought to be faced, but the group is avoiding them?

When there is a problem, the leader needs to formulate the right question and inject it at the right time:

"Jane, what are your thoughts on this?"

"Harry, how did you feel when Jack disagreed with your idea?"

"Joe, were you aware that three times you cut off others when they were speaking?"

"Kathy, I noticed you were annoyed or bothered with Sarah. Why?"

The Goal of Christlikeness

The objective of the questions is to help the group and its individual members both take responsibility for what is happening and to grow more like our Lord in learning to respond and help others. Usually, each person is too wrapped up in themselves to see others. Through nondirective leadership, you are giving people the opportunity to be themselves, to take responsibility for how they affect others, and to learn more Christ-like ways to relate to others and to handle problems.

These lofty goals are a far cry from "sensitivity training" that can damage people by exposing weak points to the group. The whole objective is to build, not destroy.

The best way to learn this method of leadership is to take a course that teaches nondirective leadership. Such a course will actually use it so that you can experience it as a participant and learn by observing how the leader does it. The second best way is to participate in a group or project or camp that is using it. In these contexts, you as the learner can ask questions of the leader as well as observe how he handles the group.

When learning this method of leadership, be sure to learn it from the Christian perspective and from skilled leaders. This method can be quite damaging to participants if done in the wrong way. For example, the group is never permitted to criticize or to "jump on" or "destroy" another member. Most of the criticism should be only toward one's self. The leader must be careful to protect the sensitive person from the nonsensitive. The purpose of this approach is to build, not to destroy.

Jesus often used this method with the disciples. When they reached an impasse, he would step in:. "What were you discussing? (he already knew, but he wanted to get them to think and to take responsibility)" After the resurrection, Jesus left the disciples alone to figure things out, but then he would appear again to get them back on the right track. Jesus used this with those that were more mature. He used it to stretch his young leaders.

73

MAKING IT LIVE IN MY SITUATION --
QUESTIONS TO PONDER
(Mistakes of a leader and Approaches to leadership)

Group or personal:

Review the major mistakes that leaders make.

◆ Have you ever made of these? What were the results?

◆ Have you been under a leader who made any of these errors? Did it hurt his ministry or the confidence of those he was leading?

How would you rate yourself in being able to successfully lead with each of the three different approaches to leadership?

Have you ever experienced the nondirective approach? If so, share additional insight you gained from your experience. What problems do you see with this approach?

11   How to Motivate
        Others -- 15 ways!

(15 different techniques that can work for you!)

You can use these SAME motivational methods with any team, as a leader in any context, as a teacher in school, or as a supervisor in a large corporation. Most of this section is directed at the counselor to children, but they are universal principles. You will need to make the applications to your own context. The more you master these methods in your context, the better you will be equipping yourself for years to come.

A leader who cannot motivate his followers is not a leader.

WHAT IS MOTIVATION?
All motivation must involve some level of emotional response. Motivation is simply a desire to do something. The stronger the desire, the more   a person will press to do it.

It is NOT necessarily talking someone into something, or maneuvering/tricking someone into doing OUR will. In a good sense, it is helping campers WANT to do what will benefit them most.

How can you help children WANT to do what will benefit them the most?

I. Put those together who will motivate each other.

One stick on fire set next to another stick on fire will create more than double the fire of the two sticks. If I am excited about something, and my friend or partner is excited, our mutual interest generates more interest. The fire grows much bigger. In a group of 10 to 20 kids, this fire of interest and enthusiasm between two or three will spread to the others.

THEREFORE: Be careful how you group the kids for the projects, activities, games or contests.

Put the positive thinkers together, and then encourage the others to follow their lead.

Do NOT put a problem or "Dud" with an Exceller. The negative one will destroy the motivation of the positive one. In the same way, do not put a Complainer with a Driver, or a Lazy with an Energy.

II. "This is the way we do it here."

To motivate campers to follow the rules of the camp, explain each rule or expectation or tradition with an attitude that says: "Everyone does it. It's just part of this camp." From the camper's viewpoint, it is not a matter of "should I or should I not", or "can I get away with it." You present the rules in a way that says: "This is the way it is here. And doing it this way makes this a great place. We are going to work together to make this the best week yet!" The group member will want to be part of the "in" group by doing what others do.

Using this method will create a camp spirit. You are creating an atmosphere, a status quo that will motivate pride in our camp, our project, our group, and our objectives. This is part of "making expectations clear " from *How To be a Successful Camp Counselor.*

Part of the skill in using this method is your knowing <u>exactly</u> what you want. Have it very clear in your own mind exactly what is realistically expected, and what kind of spirit you want to create. With this as a clear goal in your own thinking, keep going toward that goal by expecting campers to follow you.

Remember, YOU are setting the example. YOU must be following the rules and having this spirit.

III. | **Establish high standards of excellence**

As you examine the ministry in which you are serving , where do you see high standards of excellence? Each camp is unique, but in what does your camp excel : buildings and grounds, program, staff, music, Bible emphasis, leadership, spirit, Holy Spirit results?

When campers come into this <u>environment</u> of excellence, many are motivated to rise to the challenge -- to excel like everything around them.

Challenge them to be their best, do their best, and achieve their best. Then <u>believe in them,</u> enjoy them, and work alongside them. (1) Your challenge to them, **(2) your example**, (3) your confidence in them and (4) this environment is a WINNING combination.

Therefore: Don't feel bad about demanding the best in whatever you are leading them to do.

79

If you don't do this, you are letting your campers down.

Sometimes, when you expect a lot, they will gripe and grumble. Their griping and grumbling does NOT mean that they don't want it. The old nature just does not like to put forth effort.

Your being tough means that you care-- and they will respond!

Sometimes this can mean holding the line with appropriate discipline. (see that section on discipline in your manual)

Word of caution: construct the challenge, the standards and the rules so that they can be obtained. Setting it TOO high can cause a reverse reaction. That is why we need to KNOW our campers, so we can know how high a goal is realistic.

Using this motivational method ASSUMES that you are communicating with your campers. It ASSUMES that you have established a good relationship with them. You need to get this message across to both individuals and the group.

IV. Use Group Cooperation and Enthusiasm!

1) Put together those that will generate enthusiasm, and this will drive the whole group. (See #I above)

2) EMPHASIZE cooperation , team spirit, and "We **can** do it together." The emphasis on teamwork should be predominant (as opposed to individual achievement). In any group of 100 youth, many times you will find that only a few have experienced success or some special rewards. The Lord's emphasis on unity in John 17 has this element of teamwork. There is too much competition between

youth ; now it is time to balance it by giving prominence to working together (which requires having a concern for others).

3) When possible, team campers up to do things together. Each will motivate the other to follow through. There will also be an element of competition. No one wants to be the weak link that hurts the others.

4) Generating this spirit also generates group pride. When a person in a group catches this kind of thinking, he will have a strong desire to keep up with the others and to do his part. It is like the kid who is up to bat, he wants to hit a home run for his own accomplishment, but he is also VERY conscious of his teammates who are either on the bench or on the bases.

5) If the group norm becomes one of excellence, or effort, or "never die," or "never quit," then the group will generate its own enthusiasm to maintain that norm. As a counselor, jump on this bandwagon and reinforce this norm with encouragement.

6) An individual group member may be lagging in zeal to do a task, or to do his part, but he will push himself to achieve for the sake of the group.

7) When you, as the leader, are obviously devoted to the group (you have the group's best interest at heart), campers will not only accept, but appreciate your pushing them to achieve and to do their best.

Remember: If you are hard on the campers, you must get the message across that is NOT for your convenience or pride; you are doing it for them because you care.

V. Expect the best from every follower.

The human tendency is to live UP or to live DOWN to the expectations of those over us or around us.

You communicate your confidence (or lack of it) in your tone of voice, your posture, your facial expression, your touch, and in your attitude toward each person under your leadership.

As each does a project or plays a game, as you encourage each, assume he/she will do his best.

Even though you must keep an eye on campers, don't be a guard at the bank. To prevent problems, be where the campers are, but **keep a positive attitude,** and in manners and motions assume each will do his best.

Look for the best in each person, try to put that person where he can succeed, and then expect success. BUILD ON HIS STRENGTHS.

When you work with each of your campers, you can't fake it. You need to honestly believe in them, see that spark of possibility, visualize that untapped potential. Most people operate far below their potential, simply because they do not believe they can rise any higher.
Some kids are obviously talented -- don't let their pride keep you from praising them.

Some kids have their talent covered up with all kinds of weird behavior or unattractive physical appearance.
LOOK DEEPER.

Remember: Everyone is changing. This group we call youth is changing very very fast. Believe in each one that he / she CAN change for the better -- with motivation. YOU may be the spark that ignites their potential!

Everyone wants to achieve, to be somebody, to make a mark, to count, and you can put a person in high gear if you set him on that road to do just that.

But as a counselor, also be ready to pick him up if he falls.
Even when a child does not believe in himself -- don't quit assuring him that you do.

Motivational comments to a camper:
"You have great potential."
"You did very well at _____ "(project or activity)
"You caught on quickly to _____"
"I know you have had a tough time, but I believe you can do it."

VI. | **Learn what they want; then show them how they can get it .**

This method works better when working with older youth such as college students.

It can apply to short range goals (i.e. making friends) or long range goals (i.e. vocation).

Tying into life long goals may be too big for one week at camp with children or teens. . Probably, you will not learn this with most campers (most do not have these defined yet). But if you CAN find out what it is, you have a key to motivation.

83

Relate what we are doing to his goals (short term or long term), his needs, his desires.

Show them how they can meet some of their basic needs. But perhaps their attitude or action is getting in the way. Perhaps lack of cooperation or obedience is destroying what they really want to have. Many times a person will have a mannerism or habit that is interfering. But the y do not see how they are drilling holes in their own ship! You can motivate others by gently explaining what may be so obvious to you but not seen at all by them. Here are a few basic desires that most youth want to fulfill:

1. They want to have fun.
2. They want to have friends (to be liked by others).
3. They want to achieve.
4. They want to improve, to become good at it.
5. They want to learn.
6. They want to grow up.
7. They want to be trusted.

Find out what they want (the above list) , and then relate what we are doing to how it will help them to get what they want.

If a person clearly knows what he/she wants to do, that in itself will create a driving force that will inexorably drive the person in that direction.

ENCOURAGE them to keep going toward their goal. Do not let them quit. Many are used to giving up when it gets hard. Their goal may be immediate, or short term or life long, but is motivating. Keep them focused on it.

VII. | **Breaking into a new area of learning.**

or solving a problem -- crashing through a barrier --- is very motivating.

This can be the same idea as creating a challenge, and then moving through the steps toward conquering that challenge. Some camps try to structure their staff responsibilities to continually challenge returning staff with new responsibilities.

Some youth take lots of encouragement to keep going until that final break through.

To use this method, you might have to step back and take an overall view of the total camp experience for those under your leadership. What IS new? What IS a challenge? You may have to create one!

VIII. | **Use failure itself as a motivator.**

Create an environment where failure is not fatal!

Two ways to **prevent** a camper's failure in a project:

1) If you see him doing something that is going to destroy his project, interrupt his progress by asking questions that will put him back on the track.

Example: "Before you put those two things together, wasn't there something else we were supposed to do? What step are you on in

the instructions? #6? Show me what you did for step #4 and #5. "
(You know he skipped #5)

<u>You are not doing the project for him or taking over,</u> but you are
preventing a disastrous failure.

Note: To do it FOR him will surely <u>destroy</u> all motivation.

The "slower" the child, the closer you need to watch this, but it
DOES happen with even the brightest children. Some who are more
disorganized may move ahead without following the
success-established sequence of steps.

2) Like an athletic coach, some situations call for yelling at the
camper in such a way as to give the messages: "You WILL succeed,
you CAN do it, and I DO believe in you. So you CAN'T QUIT!"

WHAT TO DO IF FAILURE HAPPENS ANYWAY

1) Guide the person or the group to rethink what they/he did,
and then rethink how it SHOULD have been done. Maybe there will
be a next time.

2) Go back and tackle the problem again, with a determination
to beat it.

3) Rearrange the schedule or activities so that SUCCESS can
be experienced and morale can go up again.

4) Tell them an example of your own failure and how you
worked through it and finally recovered.

IX. | **Build success upon success** |

Once a person has succeeded, there is an unbelievably strong desire to do it again. Part of the reason is that people want to be consistent winners. One success means they have started down the road to repeated successes.

As a leader, once a person has made a small success at something, you can build on this to encourage further success:
"You did great on that project yesterday, so I really believe you can handle this one, too."
"Remember how scared you were when you first .... and remember how it was 'nothing; you did it! Now you face a bigger challenge, but you can handle this one just as you did the other one."

Keep building on what an individual or your group has already achieved. Use each success to encourage excellence or success at the next task. Because he now has his own success story, you are building the idea into his thinking that he is a winner.

You want your campers to focus on their successes, not failures. When they are feeling down or discouraged or afraid, bring their focus back to a previous success.

Note: When Israel in the Old Testament was "down," quite often the prophets would go back and rehearse what God had done for them before. Because they were successful before when they followed God, they could be successful again if they would follow God.

You want to call to the person's attention exactly what he did that made him succeed:

87

"You were discouraged at first, but you stuck with it."

"You saw the others do it, so you told yourself that you could do it too, and you did!"

"You studied hard to be sure to know your part"

"You followed the directions carefully and reread the parts that were more difficult."

"You practiced and practiced, and when the time came, you did it well!"

"You prayed and asked God to help you, and He did!"

The negative side of this principle:

Success may be seen by the individual in relationship to others. Others did it better, faster, easier, with less fear. Or maybe he looks at the "greats" and then looks in the mirror and thinks: "What a dud." This negative way of looking at one's potential can be devastating.

How do you handle a person who sees personal success is not reachable? Two options:

(1) It might be best to ignore it. You will never talk the person out of it. And calling attention to it may only deeper the person's negative feelings.

(2) To counter these low ideas of self success, use the methods of motivation being suggested and do not call attention to the hopeless comparison of the "greats."

X. Recognize the successes that are made by each person

This means that you, as the leader, will have to be keenly aware of what is happening to your followers. If your camp has some type

88

of skill classes , check with those instructors to see how your camper is doing, and then communicate the good report of success. If you have students in counselor training or new counselors or staff, this concept is important to implement. They need to know that you noticed their successes.

> Be aware of achievements in other areas. For example:
> He kept his temper when he was wronged.
> She was kind when others may have retaliated.
> He went out of his way to help another.
> She stayed behind to be with the girl that was alone.
> He set an excellent example in table manners.
> She really has improved in ....

XI. | **Tell them good success stories.**

YOU are a success. You are a counselor in this camp. How did you get here? Were you ever discouraged? What obstacles did you have to overcome?

If you have learned the life stories of some of the great missionaries or evangelists, tell them how these men did it.

Along the way, collect stories about campers that overcame obstacles, campers that were ordinary kids that did extraordinary work.

Tell Bible stories of those who succeeded when it was hard.

The idea behind stories is: They did it, and you can do it too.

Success stories reach our heart, and not just our heads.

89

They have a way to powerfully stir our feelings and change our attitudes.

There is little motivation without an increase in emotion. Stories can increase that emotion.

XII. 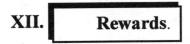 Rewards.

The proverbial "carrot" is the idea of saying that if something is done or accomplished, there is a specific reward waiting. This is the motivation of the diploma, award, certificate, and trophy. But it can also include a financial bonus or prize.

To get a camper "over the hump" of discouragement or fear, it may <u>occasionally</u> be appropriate to offer an ice cream cone at the snack shop or a special item from the gift shop if he completes the task or does particularly well.

Warning! Use this one sparingly.

4 cautions to observe when using rewards.

1. Do not offer a reward for every achievement. It will actually backfire and DEmotivate the camper.

2. Be careful not to appear to play favorites. But most of the group should understand this one camper's need for an extra shove.

3. Payment for a job well done CAN take away the pleasure of the job itself.

4. Once a habit is established, it is harmful to praise or reward a person every time. Praise for consistency would be more appropriate.

90

PRAISE AS A REWARD

You want to convey the idea that each child is loved and accepted for what he IS, not just what he can do. So praise the EFFORT and CHARACTER that made the accomplishment possible.

Sometimes a person will put forth a strong extra effort to either please you or do well at a task. It is important that you notice this effort or improvement. Be alert! Be sure to praise this person for his/her diligence.

When two of you counselors meet together and your campers are hanging around the fringes, and you KNOW that they are picking up every word you say to each other, pretend like you are ignoring your campers and tell the other counselor what a great job your kids did at _____, and brag about them. You can get amazing results in campers; they will give you even more cooperation and effort.

Honest and sincere praise can be a powerful motivator. Do not overdue it or cheapen it.

XIII. | Use competition as a motivator. |

You will find many children who have a natural bend toward competition. Grade school and junior high age are often very competitive. Boys tend to be more competitive than girls. Second born children tend to be more competitive than first or last born.

Our society is a little drunk with competition, so beware of using this too much. It is easy for the value of the activity to get lost in the heat of competition. You want to avoid this because it actually detracts from the total positive camp experience.

How to stop competition from being destructive.

Be alert for when a camper or group picks up the competition and carries it <u>too far</u>:

1. They may sink to attempted sabotage, ridicule, sarcasm, or hard feelings.

2. If they think they are losing, they may be motivated to quit.

3. If they are winning, they may lose the value of the experience in the heat of competition -- like a ball team that does not enjoy playing the game because they are watching the score board.

If you see any of these things happening, it is time to step in and redirect the attitudes. The losing team needs encouragement, and the winning team needs to step into the shoes of the others.

Competition CAN motivate an individual or group to push a little harder, to stretch a little farther, or do a little better. This is true for adults as well as youth.

For children, if there is all-camp competition with teams, do some behind-the-scenes changes to keep the competition close. Announce accomplishments and winners at individual events, but do not announce totals until the end of the week

Just do not overdo it. The value of WHAT they are doing far exceeds the value of winning against another team.

XIV. | Esprit De Corps is motivating.

How to have it:

Esprit De Corps is that group enthusiasm that enjoys working together and winning together.

1) Reward Cooperation and a cooperative spirit with praise and appreciation.

NOTICE when one person gives up his time to help another.

when one sacrifices for another.

when one gives all he has for the group.

when one comes up with an idea to help the group win or do better.

when one unselfishly does his part, sometimes alone and without fanfare.

2) Give responsibility to your group to maintain the right spirit. Do not take it ALL upon yourself to build and maintain this spirit. If you want the group to do this, make your expectations clear. (see the manual) You will have to be very clear in your own mind as to just what you want your group to do in order to encourage each other and keep the spirit high.

3) Promote and encourage communication -- talking things over, asking questions, communicating what we are doing, asking for help. For example, a basketball team that does not talk to each other on the game floor will be working with a handicap.

4) Follow through on as many of these motivational suggestions as you can use and master. Most of them will generate Esprit De Corps.

5) ENCOURAGE MUTUAL ENCOURAGEMENT

As a counselor, you can promote this by using casual questions (that you have planned out!) during waiting times. Keep the group thinking and talking in positive terms. Keep them planning together. Keep looking for good things others have done and bring it to the group's attention. Set the example. Talk about how to encourage each other and why.

XV.   How to Overcome the <u>destroyers</u> of group motivation:

How to handle destroyer # 1: Conflict

Conflict can be totally destructive, or it can actually build morale.

Build into the group an allowance for a certain level of conflict.

There has to be room to disagree, discuss, and even argue. You need to be sensitive when to step in and stop it.

Acceptable: When two disagree, let them talk out their side of the issues and explain their viewpoint. Then interject leading questions like: "What would be best for the group? What will happen if we do not go your way? Have you taken into consideration what the others want?" A leader is not one who must always have his way, but rather one who can help the group achieve a common objective.

How to handle destroyer #2 : "There is only me."

Some campers may not be aware that there are other campers, other groups, and other needs outside of his own. A very selfish and self-centered person can be a major detriment to the group.

Some alternative solutions:

1) Take this person aside, privately, for private counseling. Restudy chapters 5 & 6 in the manual. Talk man to man, with respect and concern, and lay out straight just what you see happening because of his self-centered attitude. He does NOT see the reaction of the others or else he does not see how he is actually losing by putting himself first.

2) If you have a charactered camper who is more mature, have this person give the "me first" campers some direct

advice with some of the same information in the above paragraph. Coming from a peer can be powerful .

3) With the "me first" not around, encourage other campers to just overlook the behavior and move ahead toward excellency anyway.

How to handle destroyer #3: The complainer.

Take this person aside and let him air his grief's (NOT in front of the group!). Sympathize as much as possible with his problems, and then explain to him what he is doing to the group. If he is willing to change, fine. If he is still being stiff, just tell him that he must keep his beef to himself because it is damaging the group (as well as himself), and you will not allow it. Check out chapters 5 and 6 in the manual.

Some campers just want the attention. Others are spoiled. Others are just soft. Yes, sympathize with his problem (show that you understand where he is coming from), but also show him a better way to handle his problem.

As far as the group is concerned, they may either side with this one (and the spirit go down), or they may turn against him. It may be better to encourage the group just to ignore the complaining part of the complainer. You do NOT want to isolate him because he ought to be part of the group. But neither do you want to let him destroy the morale and motivation of the others.

How to handle destroyer #4 : Destructive Criticism

This can come from the campers (toward each other), or from the counselor or an instructor. No matter who it is from, the one who is <u>hit</u> will lose his desire to move ahead.

95

What is "destructive criticism?" When someone does something wrong (or does not understand or catch on), that person can be destroyed by comments or correction that attack him personally. This would include negative adjectives like lazy, clumsy, stupid, hillbilly, etc. The idea is that in some way this person is being insulted.

Few people respond positively to a negative insult.

Criticism must focus on what or how a person is doing something, not on the person himself or his character.

How to handle destroyer #5: Too much talk
Do not be quick to talk. Listen to understand.

Children often resist (and thus do not cooperate with) adults who talk <u>down</u> to them, talk too much, or do not listen to them. Very few adults give children a real listening ear; we are too quick to preach at them.

Assume each camper is an honored guest who is worthy of your total attention. What he says is important.

Before you give advice, ask questions and listen to fully understand the thinking of this person..

If this person is upset for some reason, it is the wrong time to give advice and counsel. It IS time to sympathize and listen.

MAKING IT LIVE IN MY SITUATION --
QUESTIONS TO PONDER
(Methods of Motivation)

Group or personal:

◆ How would you define "motivation?"

◆ Do all these methods work all the time? Why or why not? What makes the difference?

◆ Which methods have you used successfully? Give a specific story or illustration. Tell what you did and what happened.

◆ Which methods have you seen others use successfully? What did this person do that made it work well?

◆ Have any of these methods backfired on you? What happened? Why?

◆ Can you recall a time when you or another person did the OPPOSITE of what is suggested to motivate campers? What happened? (If you speak about someone else, put everything in general terms and do not name names.)

◆ How have you used rewards? Did it work?

◆ When your cabin group experienced a failure, what did you do to help them recover? What happened?

◆ Tell about a time when you were in a group situation and experienced a motivation destroyer. How did you feel? How did the group respond? What did the leader do?

97

Review

- Inherent in true leadership is the continual growth of the leader. Which methods that you have <u>not</u> used would you like to master this summer?

12 How to Stay Organized and Get Even the Big Jobs Done on Time

The key to getting the most done in every 24 hour period is running by a system of goals. Goal setting is a common administrative technique that can make your leadership far more effective and proficient. Whether you are a counselor just getting out of bed in the morning or a camp director putting together a whole summer's camping ministry, goal setting can work for you.

Step #1

What do you want to get done? What do you want to happen? What is your final destination? What is your primary objective?

You must be very clear about your main, overall objective. If you are planning an evening service, or a game time, or a song time, what do you want to accomplish by the end of the hour? If you are working on a major project (i.e. creating a new Christian school, starting a camp, planning a whole summer's camp program), then you will have a larger but more general objective. In terms of a whole ministry (i.e. camp, school, church, organization), this is called a mission statement.

Whatever your project may be, it is very imortant to clearly define exactly what you want to accomplish. Most positions in camp have this included in the job description or spelled out in counselor training.

Step #2

Break down your primary goal (Step #1) into the many smaller objectives that must be met in order to accomplish the main objective.

If you are putting together a total summer camp ministry, you will have objectives dealing with staff employment, program planning, materials acquisition, meal planning, and so forth. If you are planning a one hour program, you have objectives that deal with the elements of that program (songs, message, quiz time). Each element is a goal to be accomplished.

The larger your initial objectives (step #1), the more sub-objectives you will develop. Under each of these you will then have another layer of sub-objectives. You could picture this as an organizational chart where the top box (Step #1) is then broken down into multiple boxes, and each of these are broken down again.

This whole process will force you to think through in detail just what it will take to get the job done.

It is imperative that you **write down all your objectives**. Either use the form of an organizational chart or use an outline format (I.A.1.b.). If you cannot write down the objectives, you will not meet them. Writing them down forces you to make them clear and simple.

Step #3

Starting from your first objective, (step #1), go back to your outline and put down the time when each step will be accomplished. For example, if you are planning next Friday's evening service, you must be ready by Friday, 8 p.m. Your next level may be the songs for the service. You want the song leader to have the songs chosen, the music ready, and the visuals ready by 7 p.m. If you have special music in the service, you might put down : 1. ask them to sing - Monday, 12 noon. 2. Check on their practice - Thursday, 1 p.m. 3. Give them the time for when they are in the service -- Friday, 6:30

100

p.m. But in planning for the speaker, your schedule with objectives might be: 1. Invite Rev. Goodspeak for the 3rd week of camp -- January. 2. Confirm Rev. Goodspeak (make sure his plans have not changed) -- early June. 3. Give Rev. Goodspeak the plan for the evening services - - Sunday, third week of camp.

Step #4

At this point you (1) know what you want to accomplish, (2) have broken down the main objectives to sub objectives, and (3) have assigned a due date for the accomplishment of each objective. But you have not done anything yet! All this is just planning. If you put all this on your desk under the pile of last week's mail, you have gained nothing.

Each day check your objectives. What must be done today?

This could get confusing. If you have a large chart with main objectives in several categories (schedule, planning, personnel, etc.), and each category has a variety of due dates (from 4 months ago, to last week, to next week, to 6 months from now), it would be easy to overlook something that is due TODAY. Not only that, you must get these things done BEFORE the due date. Many items take several days or weeks to accomplish.

To unscramble a potential mess, you will need a calendar. Some folks use what is termed a "day time planner." Others use a variety of different computer programs. You could use simple index cards. No matter what the vehicle, the method is the same. Here it is. Whenever you finalize a due date (Step #3), write that date down on your calendar. If the accomplishment of that item is going to take several previous days or weeks, insert notes on your calendar in the days or weeks before the due date: "This week, work on _____. Due next week!" Start each day by checking 3 days on your planning calendar: (1) Yesterday. Did I get it all done? Is there carryover? (2) Today. What is due today? (3) Tomorrow. What is coming up? Can I work ahead?

What happens if you miss a due date and something does not get done? Put it on another date so that when that future date is checked, you will set that as a goal to accomplish.

WHO NEEDS IT?

The value of this is obvious if you have a massive job to do like planning a whole week's program for a ministry. But what if you have a ministry that basically repeats itself, like cabin counseling in camp?

If your ministry job description is basically simple, use this system in a simpler form. For example, if you are a counselor, in addition to your routine responsibilities, you might have a 3 x 5 card with this:

Day 1 = learn all camper names. Observe behavior to learn about each one. Make extra effort to come alongside the shy ones. Set objectives for each camper (see the manual).

Day 2 = Counsel with one camper today. Make sure each camper is confident of where to go and when. Give prayer requests to P.D.

Day 3 = Counsel with two campers today. Find someone to play piano to accompany me on Friday night.

Day 4 = ...(your goals will include getting the rest of the campers counseled, preparation for any classes or other leadership that will be expected, completing required forms, etc.)

If you have a few key goals for each day, you will know if they are getting accomplished. If you have a more complicated schedule, you may want some type of check-off system to keep track of what is done and what yet needs to be done. Checking off a completed goal is very rewarding, and it helps center your thinking on items that are left.

REWARDS AND PUNISHMENT

Not everyone is highly motivated, but using a system of goals and checking them off when they are done does help with one's motivation. It is a reward.

You can also schedule rewards and punishments for yourself. For example:

*If I get this done early, I'll buy myself an ice cream treat.

*If I miss this goal, no snack shop for me!

*Before I take any time off, I am going to _____(goal to meet).

*Before I spend any time with _____(a friend), _____(goal) must be done.

Be tough with yourself, and be generous too! If you have a hard time getting things done, plan some clear and motivating rewards and punishment for yourself.

What this system can do for you!

1. Not all people are highly organized. This will help those who never seem to get it all done or who forget easily.

2. This system will help you set priorities. Rather than use time on minor things, you will major in the important things. You will clearly know (out of the MANY pressing needs and demands) what ought to be done and what is worthy of your time.

103

3. This will save you very much time. Without clear objectives, we do waste a very large amount of time. You will be amazed at how much more you can get done each day and each week.

4. This will help you say "no" to distractions: friends, TV, games, social times, casual reading. These things are not bad, but they must be kept in their proper place. There is a time for everything, but that which is more fun or more social often takes priority.

5. This will keep you focused on why God brought you into this ministry. You will always be aiming in to fulfill His purposes.

6. You will know when you have done the job right. There is a great sense of satisfaction in a job well done.

7. You will not be ashamed because you forgot to do something.

8. You will be entrusted with more responsibility, which means more fun!

5 DANGERS TO AVOID

Any good thing, when taken to extremes, can become a bad thing. Beware of overdoing it.

1. Do not be so focused on getting something done, that you push people aside. Jesus was a very focused and productive person, but he always had time for those in need. . Ask God for wisdom (James 1:5) to know when to put the immediate goals aside in order to minister to someone in need. We can get so goal oriented that we lose sight of people.

2. Do not get so wrapped up in goals that you lose the fun of getting things done or of ministering to others. Goals are only a means to an end.

3. One of the joys of leadership is solving problems. Take time to put your immediate goals aside to solve problems and help others solve theirs.

4 This system can develop into too much independence. Keep that balance between independence and team work. It is good to mutually depend on each other. If you let the goals have too much control, you might find yourself being upset at those that get in the way or do not keep up.

5. Do not overschedule yourself. This system of self-organization, when taken too far, can put you into a work frenzy of pushing harder and harder to get more and more done. Live life! Enjoy!

13

How to Explain the Personal Contact Rule Without Causing Rebellion

THE PC RULE

The PC rule says that there is to be **no personal contact** between campers. This rule applies primarily between boys and girls. Usually this rule is applicable to junior high and senior high camps.

When you are giving the rules that first day, or when you have to review them later in the week, here is an approach that comes along side of the teens and sympathizes with them and yet holds the line.

I have taken it from the viewpoint that you are talking to a mixed group. It is easier if you give this "pep talk" to either boys or girls and aim it specifically at that gender. It is intended to have an edge of humor, so <u>don't take the terminology too seriously.</u>

"Some of you have noticed or will notice that there are certain 'creatures' walking around here that are quite different from yourself. In fact, some of you came looking for these unusual specimens. In our biology class, they were called 'the opposite sex,' but actually you find them much more interesting and fascinating than such a cold term describes.
"There is potential conflict between your natural interests in exploring the uniqueness of these special homosapiens and the camp rules that specifically state 'hands off' or No Personal Contact --- lovingly abbreviated No PC (personal contact).
"Why such a cold rule for such an interesting area of study? What's their problem?

"Before we give the administration a hard time over this, let's take a look at WHY they insist on this high standard.

"We need to take seriously why we are here and what you CAN gain from this week. How can we get the most out of this week spiritually AND get to know another person in a special way?

1) A girl\guy relationship, if not kept within strict boundaries, can be a serious sidetrack. Did you ever try to study English or Chemistry in high school when you knew those big baby blues with blond hair were watching you? Could you concentrate? NO WAY!

2) This person we coldly term "the opposite sex" is a very fascinating study, especially when such a study centers in on one person. But really understanding and getting to know that other person is stopped or blocked when the relationship goes to the physical level.

For guys, their first level of stimulation is visual. Just looking at a girl can turn on the jet engines. Their second level is physical -- then they are heading for outer space.

For girls, their first level of stimulation is physical. So they want it as much as the guys. But they don't realize that when they move a relationship into physical contact, they are starting to send this guy on a trip that occupies his mind, will, and emotions. --- not much left for thinking about why he is really here at camp.

3) If you keep your relationship on the nonphysical level, you can really get to know the other person as a person. Guys will learn to respect the girl as a very special and unique person who is worthy of respect, instead of thinking of her as something to be used to gain a thrill.

It's fun and exciting to get to know and understand them!

108

- What do they like and dislike?
- What are their interests, hobbies, and talents?
- What makes them frustrated or upset?
- How they react to different situations?
- How they respond under pressure,
- How do they reason and think?
- What are their values and priorities and goals?
- What are their future plans and dreams
- What is their home and family like?

You miss a whole lot when you jump from "hello" to "Hold me!"

4) When the engines of sexual attraction are turned on, all these sound and sensible principles get buried under emotions. So if all else fails, remember: It's the rules. One of the things we are learning this week is that those who succeed, who make it to the top, are those who have self discipline and obey the rules. If you don't obey the little rules, you will not come through when it really counts with the big things in life.

Here are a few suggestions for those who want to find the right guy/gal:

If you WANT quality in the other person, you need to BE quality. Like attracts like. Girls, if you want the guy to respect you as a person, you need to demand that respect:
    1) Dress modestly. Give the message: "I'm not for sale."
    2) Demand hands off -- you are not a play thing.
    3) Expect affection by courtesy, kindness, thoughtfulness, gentleness. Physical affection is a cheap counterfeit without these.
    4) Make him wait. Some guys know how to play the game and fake it on points (2) and (3), but they uncover their real motives when they want to move in too soon. A real treasure takes patience to

find. If he doesn't want to wait, -- he just wants self gratification. Tell him to get lost.

Guys, if you want the girl to be attracted to you:
1) Treat her with respect and good manners.
2) Be the kind of guy that will not embarrass her in any way.
3) Be a good listener. Talk less.
4) Just as you want her to be interested in your interests, learn to develop an interest in her interests.
5) Do not crowd her. Give her room to have girl friends. Do not be so stuck on her that she can't get away from you. Too much of a good thing can turn a person off (even if the good thing is you!).

Respect is lost when the relationship turns to lust. But nothing is lost by <u>building</u> a real relationship on the nonphysical level.

MAKING IT LIVE IN MY SITUATION --
QUESTIONS TO PONDER
(The PC rule and Staying Organized)

Group or personal:

◆ Why do you think there is a need for a PC rule in the camp?

◆ What are the best and what are the worst ways of enforcing it?

◆ Will the method suggested work? Have you ever tried it? Will it solve all problems?

◆ Should there be a PC rule applied to the staff? Why or why not?

◆ Which of the steps in Staying Organized did you find the hardest to follow?

◆ **Project**: Get set for success. Put it into practice.

1) Develop a simple note card system for daily goals. If you know what will be due each day, write it down. If you do not know, leave some blanks or take guess.

2) Have your supervisor assign a larger project (i.e. plan a game time, plan an evening service,etc). Then develop a full plan on how and when you will get the job done. Use either notebook paper and outline it, or develop your own system that follows the suggestions in this chapter.

3) When you are done, exchange outlines with someone else. Each is to find things that may have been left out on the other's plans.

4) Either after step (3) or after your project has been checked by a supervisor, revise it to make it the best and usable.

111

How to Be in Control of the Group You are Leading

14   How to Lead In Front of a Group

(When it's your turn to be up front!)

There is more to leadership than standing up in front of people, but sooner or later a leader does find himself in front of people --- teaching, preaching, explaining, singing, talking, or entertaining. For most people, the thought of getting in front of others for any reason is terrifying.

Have you ever wondered, "How does he doit? He seems so relaxed!" Or maybe you have mixed emotions about when your turn comes: you are excited and scared at the same time. You want to try and yet you don't.

If you will follow the basic principles that are about to be given, you will be able to handle being in front of most groups whether adult or children or teens. Do not skip steps. Every principle is essential. It is easier than you may have ever realized (my apologies to those fat text books that teach this same thing!).

I. **Be prepared.**

There is no substitute for preparation. If you are telling a story, KNOW that story. If you are preaching, practice that message at least 8 times. If you are leading songs, have the music ready for yourself and the instrument as well as the order of songs and which verses will be used.

Many times a leader is working with a wide time variable. You do not know how long the song section will take, or how long the game will last or how long the message will be. The solution is to always prepare 25% to 50% MORE than you think you will need. Then watch the clock during your up-front leadership time and simply cut out what is needed to stay within the time frame allowed. **It is far easier to cut out extra than to find yourself with 10 minutes to go and nothing to do!**

II. **Relax and enjoy it.**

If you are a leader, you probably enjoy being in front of a group and doing your thing. Whether or not you have a natural tendency to enjoy it or dread it, the group will follow your lead. If you are nervous, they will be. If you are enjoying yourself, they will enjoy this time. If you "have it together," they will give you a positive response.

Easier said that done! "How do you do it? My stomach is in knots and my tongue will not work!"

The key to relaxing in front of the group is to have a purpose for being up in front. You have a mission, a goal, a zeal to help the group accomplish something or respond to something. When you stand up in front, you are not thinking about your knocking knees or the sour face in the third row. You have ONE thing in mind: how to bring the group along with you to reach that goal. A few examples:

When preaching, you have a message from the Lord. You have the awesome privilege to teach the very Word of God! You want these people to reach new heights or get victory in the Lord or find the answers to life in Jesus Christ.

When song leading, your objective is to create musical worship, or to bring the group together to just enjoy singing, or to create a special fun time.

When leading games or a fun activity, get wrapped up in creating memorable times.

This is another key: "You" the leader don't count! You are lost in what you are doing. Everyone's focus of attention is on where you are taking the group, not who is taking them there. When YOU are focused on the goal, you are directing the groups focus on that goal (and OFF the leader). If you see someone looking intently in some direction, it's natural for you to look in the same direction to figure out what is of interest. That's exactly what happens in group dynamics.

The next key to making it all happen is prayer. Whatever your purpose or task in front of the group, if it is a good purpose, drown your preparation time and presentation time in prayer. It is not just asking God to "bless this mess;" it is asking God to give you the contents of what you are doing. Pray over the message and what to include or exclude; what songs to sing and what verses to include; what games to play and how to explain them. Let God have a vital part in the planning process. Ask God to take you over and do it through you. Even while up in front, continue asking the Lord to do it through you. Focus on Him and on your goal. In summary, here is an easy -to -remember ....

3 Point Formula for Success

Adequate preparation + adequate prayer + zeal for your purpose = a relaxed and confident leader.

115

III.

> **Use good platform manners.**

Platform manners -- what they are and how to use them to command attention.

1.. SPEAK UP! If you are outdoors, you might have to shout. If you are in a large room, you need to force more volume. If you are using a microphone, speak very clearly, don't eat the microphone or play with it, and don't blast your audience out.

Speaking clearly is very important. Work on cutting each word: make every syllable very distinct. Do not talk too fast. It is better to talk too slowly.

Avoid the monotone (an easy trap if you are nervous!). Use variety.

2. Use body language.

SMILE! If you expect them to smile, you must set the example. Enjoy the experience, and your group will enjoy it with you. Give the visual message that you are doing O. K.

Use your hands to do something. Hold onto something. Use them for gestures. But do NOT fidget with them -- wrong message!

Stand tall and straight. Walk around. Hang loose with those long limbs.

Keep the feet flat on the floor or moving. NOT resting on one ankle.

The toughest thing to do in front of a group is to make your body cooperate and give a positive message. The solution is back with

116

the previous points: relax, and get into the goal. Let your body direct the focus of attention on the purpose of your mission.

3. Be ENTHUSIASTIC!!

Work on getting "into" what you are doing. Preaching -- get excited. Singing -- get excited. Leading games -- get excited. LOVE what you are doing. Demonstrate that you are sold on what you want others to do.

IV. | **How to handle THE 5 MAJOR distractions.**

Assuming you have done everything you should for preparation, and assuming you are excited about your mission and are ready to bring the group along, what do you do when there's trouble that you could not prevent?

1.   Nonparticipation: They just are not following.
♦ Do not let it get to you. If the group picks up your nervousness or aggravation, that message will work against you.

♦ If preaching, speaking or story telling, (1) shorten it up and end it, or (2) put more life into it.

♦ If leading games, activities or songs, (1) keep it moving, (2) end the game/activity when interest starts to fade, (3) move ahead to a different one, (4) adjust the schedule so less time is spent on this part of the program.

♦ Move to another activity or segment of the program and use a different leader.

117

♦ Draw it to a conclusion if circumstances are against you: the group is just too tired, or it's too hot, or what you are doing is of little interest.

2.   The lemon face: Reading his/her face tells you that you are doing it all wrong.

♦ Do not let this person kill all that you have worked and planned and prayed to accomplish. This person has put nothing into this hour and plans on getting nothing out of it!

♦ Concentrate on those faces that are with you. Look for a smile.

3.   The talkers: they are running their own little program, usually in the back left row.

♦ Your main concern is that this little group is distracting the others. Plan ahead for another leader or helper to talk to or sit next to this group.

♦ Sometimes it is effective just to stop, stare, and say nothing. Remember, the whole group will follow your looks. If you do this, do NOT do it in anger or aggravation. You are simply correcting misbehavior.

♦ Say something. Usually just a word of reminder. "Girls in the back row, may I have your attention, please.?"

4.   The noisy or visual distraction from outside the group.
   ♦ It may be a clap of thunder, a loud truck, fire whistles, a chair that falls over, a door slams,..........
   ♦ Think fast. Can you make a quick joke about it? If not, just say something about it, and then get back with your topic. By

118

drawing everyone's attention to it, you have the group following you, so they will follow you back to your topic.

5.. The antagonist.

You may be leading a discussion. You may be having a question and answer time after a presentation. You may be moderator of a meeting or committee. You may be speaking when this person interrupts you! No matter what the situation, someone is facing you who disagrees with you in front of others. And <u>YOU</u> are the leader!

Let's first consider who this person may be. The antagonist may

......
      simply have a question.
      have missed your point or misunderstood you.
      disagree with you and everything you have said!
      have different goal.
      have a different philosophy or a different theology.
      be very emotionally involved, upset or even angry.

What should you do?

First, do nothing!

♦ Do not interrupt as this person spills out his problem or gripe or complaint.

♦ Do not react in any way. Maintain a <u>blank</u> expression, but <u>do</u> show interest and attention (i.e. respect).

♦ Do not defend yourself or attack him (more on this later).

♦ Do listen very carefully and put your brain on the fast track. Be answering these questions mentally as you continue to listen or as you pause before giving a response.

119

1. Where is this person coming from?
Different philosophy or goals?
Anger? Past hurt or injustice?
Fear? Envy? Pride? Selfishness?

2. Does this person have a (or any) valid points?

3. Is there a misunderstanding? Missed points? Wrong information on your part or his?

4. What does he want you to think or do? (He may or may not know)

Second, after hearing him out *, you need to respond. The response is totally dependent on the person and the situation. There is no substitute for your own mature judgment at this point.

(* Note: Occasionally you have an upset person or a nervous person that will just rattle on and on. You will note with this type that he will slip into a "repeat" mode and keep saying the same thing. After you have heard it all once, politely but firmly interrupt him: "Mr. Smith, Mr. Smith, a, Mr. Smith, thank you for your comments, now please allow me to respond.")

1. If it was a rude interruption during a presentation, you have at least three options:

♦   "Thank you for that comment" or "Thank you for your interest" or "I can understand why you feel so strongly about that."

♦ If the audience or group is annoyed with the interruption or is not in sympathy, make a brief comment or light comment and then move on.

120

◆ "Thank you for your concern. I'll handle that afterwards."

2. If the question or issue is one for which you are not prepared or do not have an answer:

◆ "I'm sorry, but I do not know."
◆ "I'll check on that and find out."
◆ Call on someone else who is there who may have the answer or information.
◆ "Can you tell me a little more about that?" Turn it back on the questioner.

3. If the question/comment is irrelevant to the topic at hand:

◆ "That is another issue that we cannot deal with at this time."
◆
◆ You may want to set up a meeting or procedure to deal with it another way or at another time.

4. If you are caught because you are either not prepared, you overlooked something, or you are just wrong:

◆ "Thank you for that insight. I missed that."

◆ "Can you give me more information on that later? I did not know that part of it."

◆ "I stand corrected. You are right."

5. If you disagree with the antagonist:

◆ Thank him for the parts of his comments with which you can agree.

121

- Compliment him on his strong point: insight, research, clear thinking, memory, concern.

- Know why you believe or stand for what you do, and then explain your position. Very often you have thought something through while the person objecting has not. Be prepared to defend your position or decision or plan.

- You may have to conclude with this: "I think we shall have to agree to disagree. I firmly believe _____ and do not think it wise to change. Thank you for understanding my position."

Throughout the whole exchange, you must stay very calm and in control. The calm person is always the victor, and the angry person always the loser. You are the leader, so you must demonstrate the finest in leadership qualities. The antagonist can do about anything because he has nothing to lose (except group support for his position), but you must maintain the respect of those that are following you.

A word about **what to wear.**

- It is better to err on the side of dressing UP too much instead of being too casual.
- Generally, a leader will dress one level higher than his group. Dress a little better.
- If speaking in front of an adult group in a church, dress up.
- With teen groups usually sharp looking casual is in order.
- On the recreation field, if you are going to get dirty with the kids, dress for it. Otherwise, dress one step higher.
- If you want the respect of the group, dress as though you expect it.
-

How to lead songs

15

when you are not a song leader

As a Christian leader you are sooner or later gong to find yourself in front of a group with a song book in your hand. Maybe you are cornered into leading songs in a youth group, evening service or in the dining hall in camp. If you just do not get this thing of song leading, such situations can be extremely uncomfortable. Let's see how to live through it with some sense of success. This section assumes that you are NOT into waving your hands, keeping the beat, or even reading music.

I. If you can come up to the ideal, do it. Learn the professional way to beat out the timing with those tricky waves of the arm. Learn how to change the tempo, change the key, change the timing, break the group into parts, and actually read the music. If you have the God given ability to go this far, the Lord expects you to develop your talents. The rest of this chapter is for those who just don't "have it."

II. PLAN the music program ahead of time. Whatever methods from this list you choose, PLAN ahead. A lack of planning is a disaster if you are not well experienced at working with music in front of a group. You do NOT have to limp along. You CAN have a great song time, if you plan ahead.

III. Work with the pianist or musician. Plan the songs you want to sing, and then give a copy of the music to the musician. Ask this person (usually a pianist, but in a camp, it may be a guitarist) to take the lead and start the song when you are leading. Normally, the song leader will take the lead. By working together, no one will know!

123

This is how it works: You introduce the song, the pianist plays the introduction, have the pianist play a <u>louder</u> first note or down beat, and you are off! You just sing along with the rest of the group. Don't wave your hands or even try to fake it. Just smile and make it appear that you are enjoying this song (even if you are dying on the inside from fright!).

IV. Use visuals.

♦   Hymnbooks or songbooks are great because everyone will ALWAYS look down no matter how well they know the song. That means that they are not looking at you!

♦   Song cards can be tricky. Practice holding them and turning the pages BEFORE you get in front of the group. A great advantage is that your hands are busy so you feel more relaxed. You can also point to the words on the song card to get the song started (this is in place of the usual song leaders arm/hand motions). Remember, you turn the page just BEFORE the last word in order to keep ahead of the song.

♦   Overhead transparencies. It takes more equipment and arranging as well as a dim room, but they keep everyone together. If you make these yourself, beware of copyright laws. You can use a pen to point to the words on the projector (not on the screen). You can even play "follow the bouncing ball" by tapping the pen below each word as it is sung. Do not use this last method very often.

V.   Work with someone who can help you get a good down beat. This simply means holding your hand up in the air as the attention to start (as the pianist plays the introduction) and then giving a clear downstroke on the first beat or note of the song.

124

VI. If you feel ill at ease, inexperienced, or just dumb about leading songs, do NOT relay any of these feelings to the audience. Stand up just as confident as can be and go ahead with your game plan. Remember, an audience follows the leader, so if you feel nervous about singing, so will they. This is NOT the message you want to give.

MAKING IT LIVE IN MY SITUATION -- QUESTIONS TO PONDER

(How to Lead in Front of a Group and How to Lead Songs)

Group or personal:

♦ Because of different spiritual gifts and different personality strengths, some leaders do quite well in front of a group without going through all these steps. Which ones do you skip? How could you be more effective if you put effort into the steps you are overlooking?

♦ If these steps are followed, can <u>anyone</u> be a leader in front of group? Why do you think so? What are the exceptions?

♦ Review the platform manners. What really turns you <u>off</u> toward that person up front when the leader is <u>not</u> following good platform manners?

♦ Relate how you were in a meeting and there was a major distraction. How did the leader handle it? What happened to the group's attention?

♦ Have you ever been in a cabin, during cabin devotions, and a mouse ran across the rafters or an animal was heard under the cabin? What did you do?

Group Assignment:

♦ "The next time we meet together, be prepared to lead a song. Use any of the methods or suggestions given. Use songs that will be sung in camp this week."

126

◆ If there is a week of counselor training, it would be well to repeat this assignment several times.

◆ For the next section on leading games and activities, be prepared to teach a new game or a game that will be used in camp. This may be a game to be used in a cabin, after lunch in the dining hall, or after supper on the play field.

16 How to Lead Games the Easy Way.

HOW TO LEAD GAMES THE EASY WAY

There are two basic types of games: sports and group. Sports would include all those games you have played in school. Group games can include parlor games, guessing games, evening service games, or field games like Capture the Flag.

OPTIONS FOR HOW TO DIVIDE THE PARTICIPANTS INTO TEAMS:

- Have all the boys on one side, and the girls on the other (usually does not work)

- Have a list of all participants and plan ahead who will be on which team. Do this with someone who knows all the participants so the teams are equal.

- Line everyone up and count off (1,2,3,4,1,2,3,4,...) by how many teams you need.

- Make a game out of lining up to count off: tallest to shortest, or oldest to youngest, or by birthday month. The group must do this without help from the leader (if they are old enough).

- Choose two of the best players and have them choose the teams. (Problem: poorest players are chosen last, and that hurts. Avoid this problem by privately instructing them to choose the smallest first.)

- Choose two adults to choose up teams (que them in ahead to choose the youngest first).

BASIC PRINCIPLES TO FOLLOW
WHEN IT IS YOUR TURN TO LEAD GAMES

◆ Involve all the campers. Try to avoid games where most participants are either on the sidelines or inactive.

◆ Be flexible. Changes in weather, in available leadership, in facilities available, in number of participants can all change the way an activity will work. Be ready to adjust.

◆ Be over prepared. Plan for at least 30 minutes more activity than you think you will need. This will give you the added resources in case some games do not go over well or in case things move along much faster than you anticipated.

◆ Be positive and up. No matter what happens, just adjust and move ahead. Do not let a failure or a negative attitude on the part of the group get you down. You are the leader; so set the example for what you want from the group.

◆ Consider the needs of the group. Plan games/activities that fit the age, the climate, the energy, the ability, and the knowledge of the group. Three p.m. in July is not the time for Capture the Flag.

◆ Plan games/activities that fit your physical situation. If you have 40 acres of woods, figure out how to use it. If you have only a soccer field, plan things that will make the best use of it.

WHEN YOU ARE THE LEADER OF A SPORT ACTIVITY:

◆ If you are in charge of leading a sport, find a manual with all the rules. It might be well to talk with those who have done it

130

before to learn what rule adaptations are common for this particular camp or setting. Know the rules.

◆ When starting a sport, most of the kids will "know" the rules, so explain to them those parts that are either adaptations or are often misunderstood. For example, in playing softball, you will need to clarify the rules on how to pitch, if there is stealing bases, when can a runner leave a base, and who determines "safe" or "out." Carefully think through any sport before getting out on the field or the court to lead it.

◆ A normal sport can turn into a group game by your creative use of alternatives. For example, in softball, you can change the rules so all the boys have to run backwards, or every runner must hold onto a partner, or all adults have to hit left handed. How about having all the normal rules EXCEPT run the bases backwards so that 3rd base is first base. You can create memorable moments by thinking up a few strange rules to change the whole game.

When leading games, apply all the principles from *How to Lead in Front of a Group*.

HOW TO TEACH A <u>NEW</u> GAME OR ACTIVITY -- step by step

◆ Do NOT tell the group ahead of time what they are going to do.

◆ Bring the group to the playing area.

◆ Divide up into teams, as needed. (see above suggestions)

◆ If the game permits, you may want to position the players of one team so you can walk them through the steps of playing the game.

- If the game permits, give them a demonstration of how to play. (example: ping pong, dodge ball)

- If the game is more complicated, explain ONE step at time how the game is played.

- If possible, do not tell them what they are playing, unless the title or description would ignite their imagination and interest. (Example: Gold Rush!, Russian Spy Chase!)

- Do not allow too many questions at this point. It is better to get right into the game and coach them through it.

- For more complicated games (like Capture the Flag), have them play for a designated period of time, then stop the game, call them all together, and give them a pep talk on some alternatives, strategies, or reminders of the rules that you saw being broken.

- Be sure to have enough referees or supervisors in or around the playing field. These people need to have had a private session earlier on how to play the game and all the rules.

- Watch the stages of the game: (1) no interest because of no knowledge or confusion (2) Initial interest , "Let's try it, maybe it will be fun" (3) Real interest as they get "into" the game. (4) Peak interest and peak energy output. (5) Fading interest. Either they are losing, getting tired, or the game begins to lose it's fun content. (6) No interest. The game is worn out or has turned negative.

- STOP THE GAME as close to the end of (4) as you can measure. Stopping at this point should evoke some "Do we have to quit?" kind of responses. Stopping at this point will

132

leave the desire to play it again. If you play until (6) is
reached, you have killed a good game.

♦ As quickly as possible, move into the next activity.

HOW TO PLAN A GAME TIME

♦ Use resources to plan your game time. Spend time in books
and magazine that can give you ideas. As a game leader, you
will want to be building a library , catalog or notebook of ideas
with detailed plans.

♦ Be ready with far more games than you think you will need.

♦ Have all the props or equipment ready BEFORE the
participants arrive.

♦ Start with games that bring the group together. Ideally, you
will want to use "mixer" games that require the group to get to
know each other.

♦ Alternate between types of games: active to quiet, pen and
paper to active or thinking, large group to small group, total
participation to limited participation.

♦ If you are outside or in a gym and have had a very active and
high energy game, plan some cool down time or dead time.
Usually kids want to do nothing for a few minutes after a very
active game.

♦ Keep the program moving! NEVER be scrambling to find
another activity or find the props or find the leadership that
you need. Be ready. Do not allow any dead time (unless you
planned it for a cool down time.).

133

- *The Complete Encyclopedia of Christian Camp Directing and Programming* has many ideas and a large section of resources. *The Camp Counselor's Handbook or over 90 Games and Activities Just for Rainy Days!* is a handy little volume designed for the camp counselor or Program Director. Both can be purchased from McElroy Publishing. 800-225-0682 or 508-425-4055

Character

Traits

for

Ages 6 to 18

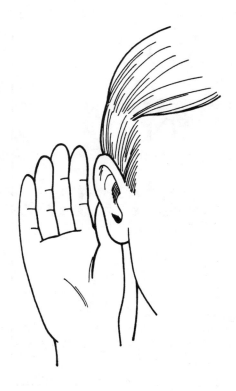

HOW TO REALLY UNDERSTAND OTHERS

This section is for the leader to sharpen his knowledge in understanding the most important people in camp -- the campers! The best use of this section would be to use it as a starting point and then add to it from one's own personal observations. The better you understand the ones for whom you are responsible, the more effective you will be. Too many leaders expect the wrong thing or do not adjust to that which is normal.

The greatest teaching tool to understand others (both campers and peers) is to learn to LISTEN.

LISTEN, LISTEN, LISTEN.

James 1:19 "let every man be swift to hear, slow to speak."

When campers are talking to each other -- unobtrusively listen. When you are just "hanging around" together, casually ask questions, and listen. Listen for what? Listen for ....

* What is important to them?   * desires
* What do they hate?   * dreams
* What is believed?   * life goals
* What do they love?   * past failures
* What is frustrating?   * visions
* What is easy ?   * people who are admired
* What is of interest?   * What do they want?
* What do they value?   * Where are they going in life?

LISTEN to gain a real understanding of the other person. This assumes that you really do care about each one.

137

Your listening in itself is a motivator because it shows you care.

To understand those under your leadership, you will also want to understand the background -- where is he/she coming from? (see chapter 16 in the manual)

The more you understand, the more you will understand the needs of the individual. The more you know the needs, the more you can pray specifically, motivate appropriately, and lead intelligently. If you listen closely enough, the other person will tell you all about themselves.

The lists that follow are all generalizations and will NOT hold true for every child in each category that is defined. Use these as a starting point and then add your own observations.

17   Enjoying Ages 6 to 11

- "WOW! Let's Go! When can we start?"
- Run, don't walk is their lifestyle. They are on the GO!!
- Be the first, be the best, have the most is the goal for boys. Competition!

- This group is ALIVE! and lots of fun.
- They have not yet developed hang ups.
- They usually don't care about self-image.
- They are not dependent upon the group (This changes in 5-6th grade for girls)
- They love to eat. "More food!" *(Do not allow eating contests.)*

- It is the age of discovery. They love to explore new things.
- They like a new challenge.
- Some think they can handle anything ,but they do not know their own limitations until IN the situation. Then they may be frustrated or afraid even to tears. This CAN be dangerous, so *watch the water activities* closely.
- When against a wall he can't get over, he may worry or complain or lie or cheat or make excuses.
- It is a great age for learning. They drink it all in.
- They want to do it all. Boys are often in high gear.

- For younger ones, hands on learning is still strong.
- Many younger ones in this age may be immature, babyish.
- You will find more homesickness in this group.

- The older ones are showing their learning styles and personality types.

- As they grow through this age , they want adults less and want the peer group more.
- They are becoming more independent.

- Age 10 is a special age (may happen between 9 and 11 chronologically).
- It is THE Ideal age: Cooperative, obedient, happy, ... Almost all positive.

- On the upper end, grade 6, some are starting to mature physically, socially, and emotionally.
- Each child, at this age, is on his own time clock.
- Some will look like 4th graders, and others will look like 8th graders.

- Girls are beginning to slow down -- sometimes.
- Girls sometimes want to be grown up with eyes on the boys and lots of boy talk, and sometimes they are just plain wonderful little girls. Consistency is not.

- *Keep this age in motion — keep them moving.*
- *Keep anticipating what is coming up.*
- Rest hour in camp?. They need it, but will NEVER admit it.
- Bedtime? Once they stop moving, they start sleeping. *Get them quiet for 10 minutes and most will be "out."*

- Those that are maturing early, will easily look on the younger ones as "babies."
- "A year or two ago" is like last century to this age.

140

Appreciating
Ages 11 to 14

(Junior high age)

- They have their adult brain ability but are lacking common sense or wisdom.
- Wisdom comes with age, and they don't' have it yet! But they don't know that they don't have it!

- CHANGE is the key word.
- Some will have bodies of adults, others will look like pencils or boards. They come in ALL sizes. They are growing fast

- They are restless and emotional.
- Many may be constantly fidgeting (boys), or talking (girls), or moving.
- Self control is hard, so *they need lots of encouragement or just reminders.*

- This age needs understanding and patience, but outwardly they fight against it.
- They are breaking from "Mommy and Daddy" into ????; they don't know what.
- They often try to be free from authority with a rebellious attitude.They want very much to be treated like an adult, so do it. But keep your expectations realistic.

- *Treat them as adults in your tone of voice, by asking for advice, by questioning them to think something through.*

- They are often peer group slaves.

- You will see them in a "pack" with two girls hiding behind another. The pack is the security --they are scared, insecure, & lacking confidence.

- "I can handle it" "I can do anything" Until in the situation , then they look for a quick way out. They may run, hide, quit, lie, or call for help.

- Each is quite able to think for himself. Therefore, keep giving him the challenge to think things through.
- *Guide him with questions.*

- They forget easily because the mind is going in many different directions: peer opinion, responsibilities, how to handle someone, what's for lunch, ...

- Daydreaming is common, and some are just spaced out.
- *Be patient and call them back to reality.*

- Their minds are going faster than you can talk.

- For boys COMPETITION! is in everything.
- Because they are physically becoming men, they very often want to "test" each other to see who is stronger, taller, braver, better, faster, tougher .....

- Pride is developing , even if it is based on lack of self-assurance.
- Pride is often used to cover up feeling of inadequacy.
- Don't try to crush the pride, because you may crush the person, instead.
- Even a proud camper needs your encouragement and praise.

- Girls are going after the older boys.

142

◆ They often get a crush on someone five to ten years older. *If the crush is on you, do not encourage it. Ignore it as much as possible. Be friendly and a little distant. You may have to be directly blunt, but gentle.*

◆ Girls often lose their purity because older boys may take advantage of younger girls. The implications are life long and tragic.

◆ For girls who start their monthly period , so comes the sharp mood swings. They can be very grumpy and irritable. but e<u>ach girl is different.</u>

◆ Early maturing boys have it made because they are ahead in most areas. Usually these boys are more confident, more stable, and more successful.

◆ Late maturing boys need lots of encouragement. *Protect them from unfair competition and from being the scape goat.*
◆ They CAN be cruel to each other.

◆ Early maturing girls may face jealousy from other girls.
◆ Generally, girls are ahead of boys and look down on the boys' "immature" behavior and antics.

◆ Consistency? forget it. Just not part of this age!

◆ Be the leader that they need.
◆ *You need to be the authority figure and need to earn their respect, but you also need to be understanding, listening, and respecting them as young adults. Don't come <u>down</u> to their level.*

◆ *DON'T BE HURT if you are on the outside* . That often happens with anyone who is an authority figure.

143

19   Challenging
Ages 14 to 18

(High School age)

The younger half of this age:

- Many still evidence many of the junior high traits.
- Some are just late maturing.
- Others may temporarily regress because of a mood swing or peer group mood.
- Socially, some are behind while in other ways they are mature.

....

- The vast difference between maturity level in boys and girls tends to fade as boys finally catch up.

- They are capable of adult level behavior.
- When given the *challenge* and the right context, they come through very well.

- Many girls generally put aside the male-type activity and want to be feminine. This often depends on peer pressure and cultural context. In some areas, being "tough" is in.
- Girls will often appear more reserved, apathetic or even lethargic in a <u>social</u> context because they want to be "mature" but are not sure just how to do it.

- Personalities and learning styles become more prominent.
- This causes some to be more independent of the group, while others still hold onto the peer group or "gang" for security.
- Those with strong Choleric or Dominant personality will <u>not</u> depend on the group.

- Those with high social oriented personalities will be more group dependent.

- This age lacks many experiences and experience.
- So their wisdom and judgment is often lacking.
- Healthy fear is sometimes less than it should be.
- *Keep this fact in mind when asking them to do something.*

- They are not good at self evaluation.
- They tend to overrate themselves (take on too much), or underrate themselves (afraid to try something for fear of failure.).

- As the hormones inject new feelings and drives into the blood stream, mood swings are common. They may be "down", negative, complaining, and quit for no apparent reason. Suddenly they are up and carefree, and WE are in a tailspin!

- Moods are often developed by the group.
- The GROUP becomes giddy and silly, and most will follow.
- The GROUP is serious and earnest about a problem, and others follow.
- Problems develop when the mood swings to silly (or rebellious) at the wrong time.

- Often this age is quite serious and capable of very intelligent conversation.
- Many enjoy matching "brains" against another.
- Often they enjoy a challenge to figure something out.

- Often they are totally wrapped up in themselves.
- Then they are unaware of those around them.
- *You may need to remind them to look for the needs and feelings of others.*

146

◆ They are not good at stepping into another's shoes. *Use word pictures to help them understand.*

◆ They are still very sensitive
◆ This is true even with increased maturity and ability
◆ Some hold onto problems (hurts) longer.
◆ They can be <u>sensitive</u> to what the peer group thinks, what adults think, what is said about them.
◆ They very much want to belong or at least not be a "reject" or odd ball.

◆ The more you *treat this age group as adults,* the better response you will get.
◆ *Challenge them – and most will pick up the challenge.*
◆ *Expect more – and they will deliver.*
◆ *Use respectful tone of voice, and attitude – they will respond.*

◆ *Keep your authority.*
◆ Even in the army, there is a chain of command and someone is in authority.
◆ *Earn respect* by being the leader they need both organizationally and spiritually.

◆ This age is as varied as you are.
◆ They are fast maturing. No generalizations cover them all.
◆ They jump from being young adults to children and back to adults again -- in seconds.

147

Birth order characteristics are another avenue to understand children. But as you study birth order traits, keep in mind that these are generalized statements that will NOT fit all children in this category. Rather, they are tendencies that seem to be based upon the pattern of parenting. First born and only children have the clearest set of characteristics. Last born children can often be identified. But with middle children, the circumstances are so varied that a set of clear traits is rarely seen.

20

Birth Order Sequence

FIRST BORN CHILDREN

First born children and only children have had a very similar experience. When they came home from the hospital (in fact BEFORE coming home!), this little one became the center of the universe. The parents gave it nearly 100% attention. However, this massive attention did not stop. Junior was praised, commended, and applauded for everything he/she did for the first time: the first giggle, the first role over in bed, the first to go off milk, the first to take a step, the first to .... the list goes on until he/she is the first to go to college! The high level of attention was matched with high levels of expectations. This combination produced some very definite characteristics.

The first born or only child......
1. Tends to conform to adult wishes.
   But this desire is so strong that this child may do so deceptively. Sometimes there is only outward conformity. O.K., call it as it is -- sneaky.

2. Thrives on responsibility, and the adult approval that goes with it. From day one, this child noticed adult approval. It now has become a way of life.

3. Tends to be more mature for his age. That's because the contact with adults has been voluminous, so it is from adults that he/she has taken the example. The other key factor is the responsibility that has been given/accepted has developed maturity.

149

4. Is reliable, conscientious, well organized, critical, serious, legalistic, loyal and self-reliant. He is an achiever.

5. Has an independent spirit that makes it hard to trust others or obey authority. The responsibility that his been part of one's life has also given a measure of self-assurance and independence. "I can handle it!" is an attitude. But as this one looks at others, there is a distrust because of a lack of confidence.

6. Needs help in building relationships with others. The independent spirit that does not trust others and can do things for himself builds walls instead of bridges in relationships with other people.

7. Has a theme song: "It's not fair!"
What isn't fair? The younger siblings don't have the strict rules, have more privileges, and are allowed to do things long before this only child was permitted to do them. Why the change? The parents are not as intense, are more relaxed, and have learned that kids are not as fragile as they thought. The other key factor is energy: As each child is born in the family, the parents have less energy to keep up and maintain strict discipline or guidance or teaching.

8. Needs private time or time alone.
Since this was number one, he/she is often not used to many other children around. So this one wants to get away sometimes. There is nothing wrong with this desire. Adults ought to understand and cooperate.

9. Needs to be given responsibility that he can handle.
You can see from the above that this one is used to responsibility. But now keep in mind that being given responsibility is the key to motivation for this person. Number one child thrives on it!

10. Needs to be appreciated and accepted for himself, not what he can do.

Achievement has been the hallmark of this child, but he/she needs to find the real "self" outside of the arena of achievement. So praise this person for character qualities and godly desires, not just actual accomplishments.

SECOND BORN CHILDREN

1. Are easy going and are NOT big on responsibility.

Because the older sibling always took responsibility, this one is easy going and glad to let the other one have it. But this means that he tends to NOT take personal responsibility -- blames others for problems.

2. Are keen on COMPETITION.

He spends his life trying to catch up to the older sibling and trying to make his place. Does he really think he can catch up? Mentally he knows better, but there is that inner drive that does not respond to reality.

3. Can be critical and fault finding.

He cuts the other one (oldest one?) down to his size so he does not look so bad.

4. Have the attitude: "I want it NOW!"

Since this child was number two, there has always been something of a battle in the home for him to get what he wants when he wants it. He learned to put up more of a fuss to get the attention that was lacking.

5. Tend to hold onto hurts or personal offenses.

This one is more feeling oriented. He needs to learn to forgive.

6. Are motivated through ENCOURAGEMENT rather than pressure or threats.

His comparing himself to the older sibling and the spirit of competition has left a mark of feeling never quite adequate or good enough. So the key to motivation is encouragement.

152

LAST BORN CHILDREN

Being the "baby" of the family, this one was rarely praised like the oldest child, and always has been overshadowed by older siblings, so he picked up a number of compensation patterns.

The youngest child .....
1. Is often people oriented and sensitive to others.

2. Is usually the clown, in an attempt to gain attention.

3. Tends to exaggerate. Thinks he can do anything. Feels he must prove himself.

4. Is often irresponsible with things because his focus is on people and relationships. Responsibility is low, but enjoyment of life is high.

5. Sometimes has a wide swing in behavior from being loving and affectionate to being rebellious, spoiled, impatient and impetuous.

6. Needs his confidence built.
So give honest praise for specific things well done.
Give a regular routine so he can experience success and order in his life.

7. Do NOT let him manipulate you into doing things for him -- he's good at this!

Basic rules when looking at the family order:
Each sibling will react to the next older one. If you wonder why he/she behaves the way he/she does, find out about the next older one. Usually the younger will do the opposite **or** be in competition with the next older.

153

All of these characteristics are general statements. Because a child may come from a different kind of family structure or parenting style, these characteristics may be strong, weak, or nonexistent.

They are ONLY generalities. Do not force all children into these molds. Many will not fit.

MAKING IT LIVE IN MY SITUATION -- QUESTIONS TO PONDER

(Understanding Others: Age group characteristics, Birth Order Sequence)

Group Discussion:

◆ The author emphasized LISTENING as the key to understanding children. What have you learned by using this basic tool?

◆ Form three smaller groups. Assign an age level to each group. (Junior, Junior High, Senior High).   Have them put together a description of common characteristics of that age group. They should draw on their past experience.   When complete, give a report to the total group and send a copy to McElroy Publishers.

Personal:

◆ Make a list of the kinds of things you will learn about your campers if you develop good listening and observation habits.

◆ Either take the lists that are given for each age group or start with a clean sheet and write your own description of each age based upon your experience.

◆ Go back over this list, bring to mind the children of this age that you have had, and put a little check mark by each quality that you remember experiencing with them.

155

- With which age group do you find it easiest to work with? Why?

- With which age do you find it easiest to relate to (build relationships)? Why do you think this is so?

- Did you find yourself in the material on birth order sequence? Put a little * by each statement that you think does fit you to some degree. Why are there statements that do not fit you at all?

- Why can you NOT count on birth order sequence or age group characteristics to give an accurate picture of the person that they are describing?

How can you, in this ministry context, help first born children? Second born? Last born? What needs do they have that you might be able to address?

How Do People Learn

HOW DO PEOPLE LEARN

Understanding how people learn is applicable to you, to your campers, to people you work with, and a GREAT help to you as you work as a leader in any context.

If you can have some understanding of how people learn, you will have more patience, and you will have more wisdom in knowing how to change your approach in order to communicate in a way that they will understand.

There are many ways to categorize learning styles, so let's consider a few basics by dividing people into two basic groups. In the first group, we find those who learn best by using their five senses. "Doesn't everyone learn that way?" Sure, but this group uses what they can see and hear to the exclusion of using logic or "reading between the lines." They take what is said quite literally or woodenly. That makes them easy targets for jokes that require NOT seeing things so woodenly.

GROUP #1 -- Learning literally. Take it the way it is.

This first type of person takes what you say at face value. It's like the little guy who was learning the game of baseball. When the coach yelled for him to run home, he ran home! When you are teaching these kind of people, they will take you seriously and not add (what you may consider) an ounce of reason. Everything is taken quite literally.

GROUP #2 -- Learning Logically. Reading between the lines.

The second group is , of course, the opposite. This group tends to read into things, to draw conclusions, to learn as much on the logic and feeling level as in normal academic ways. They see relationships between ideas, concepts and happenings. Out of this group would come a Sherlock Holmes (the master detective). Folks in this group <u>can</u> read too much into your choice of words, body action, and tone of voice.

This group may tend to visualize, to conceive ideas, to understand or believe what can't be actually seen. They use their intuition, their intellect and their imagination. They look beyond the obvious, and look for implications. "Things are not always what they seem to be."

Yes, there are many people who will be at one extreme, or the other extreme, or have some mix of both without having any extremes!

Can you see yourself as one or the other? Are you a 50/50 mix?

But there is more! There are two more categories of people who can combine anything from the above with two more distinct ways of handling information.

GROUP #3 -- The Organizers. One step at a time, in order!

The first group prefers to organize material or information in a step by step method. They tend to think in a logical train of thought. They prefer to have a plan and follow that plan, rather than relying on impulse. "Follow the steps!" is their idea of doing it right.

GROUP #4 -- The Doers. Let's just get it done!
The second group will tend to organize information by CHUNKS without any particular order to them. They are not big on

158

going step by step. They may skip steps in a procedure and still come out O.K..

When taking a test, they may start in the middle or the end, and still do well. Some may seem impulsive or even spontaneous. To others, it looks like they don't have a plan --they just jump in. "Let's just get it done!"

If you are one who thinks logically and sees relationships, how do you approach or teach a person who hears and thinks quite literally? What allowances do you have to make?

How should you handle a person who is NOT in your learning style? Each person takes a little different approach. The more YOU adapt to them (instead of expecting them to adapt to you) the more effective you will be.

Each personality type and each learning style should LEARN FROM the others. Each has strong points. As you work together, you yourself will GROW into a much better person if you learn from your teammate (co-counselor).

Instead of being frustrated with others who do not fit OUR mold, LEARN from them. Look for the positive things in which you are weak. Observe. Ask questions. Discuss. Learn techniques.

The information in this section has dealt with how people handle information that is taken into the mind. The other key factor to consider when teaching and working with a group is how each one's mind functions differently in order to take in information.

Oral learners have minds that process verbal communication well. With the ears they have understanding. If a person is real high in this area, he may have a very hard time reading (visual) and understanding. This person will do very well in listening to sermons, in listening to instructions or rules, and in listening to teaching.

159

The visual learner needs to see it. This one learns by reading, by seeing charts, by seeing an example of how to do it, by seeing pictures that illustrate. If a person is real high in this area, he may not process verbal information well. You can tell him the same thing multiple times, but it does not sink in. Show him a diagram or picture, and he has it.

Be sensitive to the visual learner when you are giving ORAL instructions. He may not understand !

Younger children and some adults are stuck with a feeling channel for learning. They have to experience their learning physically. This is a very difficult handicap for school. How can you FEEL English or math or social studies. But in gym or in shop they may do great!

Most people have a combination, but very often you will also find that most people tend to be a little higher in one of these areas. If you can find the learning channel for your campers, you will know how to communicate with each one. If you understand that THEY do not learn as you do, you will put more effort into teaching that uses all the learning channels.

For more information on this subject, read the fascinating book, *The Way They Learn* by Cynthia Ulrich Tobias. Focus on the Family Publishers.

MAKING IT LIVE IN MY SITUATION --
QUESTIONS TO PONDER

Personal

◆ Did you find yourself among some of the categories in <u>How Do People Learn?</u> How would you classify yourself?

◆ What happens when these concepts are totally ignored by a teacher or leader? Step into the shoes of the person who is trying to learn or expected to learn. Tell it from that viewpoint. Has this ever happened to you?

◆ How can you help a child in the Bible class who is very strong on the visual learning side?

◆ How will an oral learner memorize Scripture the easiest way? How will a visual learner memorize Scripture?

161

APPENDIX

HOW TO PLAN A FULL CAMP PROGRAM
(for the person who is putting together a complete camp program)

I. What is your objective? What do you want to accomplish during each period of camp?

This is the first and the most important question to answer. "To win others to Jesus Christ and help them grow in the Lord" is the basic objective of Christian camping, but as you get into Christian camping you will find that you will want a much more detailed and specific statement of purpose.

Your objective will determine everything that happens in camp. The toughest question to answer when planning a complete camp program is: "How will each element help achieve the purpose of the camp?" That same question must be asked of all your rules and procedures.

There is help with this initial step and with those that follow in the basic resource book, *The Complete Encyclopedia of Christian Camp Directing and Programming* . To plan a camp without this basic volume is like putting together a large model airplane without any instructions.

II. Evaluate your resources.

What is the financial base? What do you have to spend to put this together?
What do you have for a physical plant: cabins, dining hall, recreation field, swimming area, etc.
What do you have for help: counselors, maintenance, cooks, program, speakers, helpers.

165

When you plan the camp, plan it with what you have to work with. Adjust your plans to fit the reality of your limited resources.

III. Learn the past traditions and procedures.

If you are conducting the program of an existing camp, you need to know what they are used to doing. If you change too much too quickly, you can run into resistance. Many times the ways and traditions of the camp have been created from experience and are actually the best for this situation.

Obtain the manuals, schedules, program sheets, and plans from previous years. If there are evaluations from previous years, these are invaluable. Build on the past; don't destroy.

IV. Add the extras to the bare bones program.

Camp by its very nature should have a number of extras. Sometimes these are silly things that are just for fun. Sometimes they are special games or activities that fit this physical situation. Many times they are little extras that can be put into the program. *The Complete Encyclopedia of Christian Camp Directing and Programming* has a whole section on this area of camp. It is called "Sugar and Spice" for the extra things that add flavor.

V. Plan your training of the staff.

The best plans can go wrong if the staff is not with you. They need to know what is expected, how to do it, what to do when, and the rules for the new things that you have planned.

If possible, plan job descriptions. If each person knows just what is expected and where his/her boundaries of responsibilities lie, each person will be more secure and will do a better job.

166

Use counselor training to inspire the staff to achieve the camp objectives, to make this the best camp ever, to remind them that many campers will experience camp for the first time (staff needs to mirror that enthusiasm), and to answer the questions that will come.

If time allows, run through the daily schedule so the total staff can see how they fit in. You want your staff to be a team that is aiming toward the same goal, not tripping over each other or fighting with each other.

VI. Use evaluations extensively.

Evaluations will tell you both the strong points and the weak points.

Create them in such a way as to focus attention on the good things and not the bad.

Evaluate the staff, the program, the food, the schedule, the facilities, the songs, and the teaching.

VII. Ask questions, research and read.

Because you have had some experience in camp, you will tend to recreate what you have experienced. But there are many more possibilities. Start with *The Complete Encyclopedia of Christian Camp Directing and Programming* for an idea generator, and then add what can be learned from other camp directors, camp conventions, camp books, and camping journals. You will find many resources in this Encyclopedia.

Did you ever stand in front of a group and ask: "Do you have any questions?" As you looked at the faces in front of you, they all said the same thing --- nothing.

The dynamics of a group require the leader's skill if a good discussion is to take place. If you do not take into account these dynamics and the many factors that affect your group, probably your attempts at creating a discussion will have disappointing results. Let's take a look at the factors that either help or hinder a response.

Physical setting

A discussion can take place with formal rows (as in a church auditorium), but this set-up is the worst. The best arrangement has the participants facing each other. Using a circle, a box, or a "U" shape for seating will greatly encourage interaction.

Seating arrangement is important, but do not overlook the temperature of the place, the acoustics (can each easily hear the others), and the comfort in seating.

The physical setting should also include an elimination of distractions: smell of lunch being cooked, someone working nearby or in room overhead, visual distractions, etc.

Timing

It is easier to have a good discussion when the participants are wide awake, not hungry, not exhausted, and not time conscious (waiting for the next event). Probably, mid-morning classes would be ideal, but the cabin devotions just before bedtime or the campfire meeting have also proven to be great times.

Objectives

What do you want to accomplish in your discussion? The answers is not always obvious. To have meaningful discussion, the

168

leader must have a clear objective of what he wants to accomplish. Do you want to review material that has been covered? Examine a problem that is common to all? Generate new ideas? Evaluate? Know what you want the group to produce so that you can guide them in that direction.

Ask the right questions

There are several types of questions that leaders ask. Some of these move the group to participate, and others close down participation.

1. Quiz or test questions

This question is asked to find if the group members have picked up on present or past teaching. Except for the more self-confident members, this type of question creates fear, no matter who in the group is chosen. There is fear that (1) "I might be next," or (2) that "my answer may be wrong." Either way, most group members simply want to hide, not participate.

2. Open ended questions.

The answers to these questions are rarely wrong. You are asking for an opinion, or an evaluation, or an idea. You want to draw on the group's creativity or background or experience. You want wide participation.

3. Research questions

Assign a chapter of Scripture, a topic from camping books, or a survey question to ask several people. The assignment can be for each individual, but it works better if you have teams of two or three working together. After the research is done, regroup and discuss the results.

4) "Brainstorming" is an old technique, but still quite valuable. In this type of question, you are asking for a fast flow of ideas <u>without</u> evaluating or rejecting any of them. Usually, there is a

list being generated that all can see on an overhead, blackboard, grease board, or large tablet.   For example: "What could we do after supper?" or "How many ways are there to get everyone to Bible study on time?" After everyone has given all the ideas that pop into their mind, you can go back over the list and ask: "Which are the 5 (or 10) best ideas? Should we adapt or adopt any of these?" Now you have a centered discussion that should end in real decision making.

How to have a discussion with more than the leader talking. (How to get many involved)

* Ask the right kind of questions.

* Clearly communicate that you are going to openly accept any response. This communication includes body language, facial expression, tone of voice, and choice of words. Be warm and accepting.

* Establish a rapport and confidence with the group. They do not know you or how you will respond to them, so to play it safe, they will play dead. Ice breakers, humor, conversation, and questions that are lighter may help break down the initial barriers.

* If no one responded, call on someone. Choose a person you know, a person who thinks, and   someone who is self-confident.

* After a person responds:

1) Call on someone else immediately if there is group interest and several are anxious to respond.

2) Summarize what the person has said (in a complimentary or positive way). In that summary, use a few exact quotes from the respondent because this adds great value to what was said and thus encourages others to participate.

3) Ask for a clarification in a way that shows interest. For example: "You brought up two excellent points, but I'm not sure I understand the third. Could you amplify that a little more?"

4) Compliment the response, then ask for more. "I never thought of that, it's a good idea. Can someone else add to it?"

5) Add to what the person has said, or give an example.

6) In a positive, friendly, and challenging way, disagree with the response, or dare someone to take another view. If there is any doubt that you are still with the respondent, come right out and explain: "He has a good idea, but just to make us think this through, would someone take the other side?"

7) As the discussion progresses, as the leader, you will want to summarize or pull together or compare ideas that have been given.

* If the discussion gets too "warm" or heated, you may need to play the part of peace keeper. Very often in a lively discussion or if an emotional topic is being discussed, two or more may disagree simply because they are not "reading" each other. As the leader, paraphrase or ask for clarification and draw the two viewpoints together.

* At the end of the discussion or periodically during the discussion, summarize what has been said and the direction the discussion has gone. Many group members will not be conscious of the flow and direction. The summary helps them see the many good and positive things that have been said. This encourages more participation either this time or next time.

* There are always quiet ones in any group. Watch their faces. When they are "with" the discussion, call on them. "Kathy, what do you think?" Be sure to praise the response. These quiet ones are often deep in thought and have excellent input.

Why won't they talk?
Sometimes you can do everything right and still everything goes wrong!

Even a skilled leader cannot always get a good discussion going.

1) They don't know you. (Give them time. Do something with them.)

2) They are tired. Their brains are not in gear.

3) The subject matter is of no interest.

4) The questions are not challenging. They are too simple.

5) The questions are too challenging. They are above them.

6) They don't know what you want. Do you want their opinion, a particular answer, an evaluation, or something else.

7) They are "reading": you as uptight, nervous, insecure. So they do not feel at ease to participate.

8) You are giving the message that you really don't care. This is just something you have to do. You,. the leader, are not really into it. So they are just following you!

9) You are talking too much. You ask a question and then keep on talking, like the radio talk shows. (STOP. Silence will not hurt. Give them a chance to think.)

10) Their mind is on something else. You are forcing a topic when interest or emotion is elsewhere. (You need to change the mood of the group, or change the topic, or change the time for discussion.)

How to NOT kill a discussion

Do NOT look for the "correct" answer.

Do NOT be critical if the answer is not exactly what you want.

Do NOT go into lecture or just verbiage if no one responds.

Do NOT let the discussion ramble all over. Keep it moving toward the goal. Keep bringing members back to the main topic or question.

Do NOT let one or two kill the discussion by dominating.

Do NOT get responses from several and then give your response or idea of the best. It is disparaging to the participants.

How to inject some variety

Rather than always standing in front of the group or sitting in a circle and taking charge, try these alternatives.

1) Instead of you, the leader, calling on the next person, tell the group: "After you speak , you call on the next person to speak." It

may take a little getting used to, but with your coaching and encouragement, they will enjoy this new format.

2) After you present the topic or question or research, divide the group into two's or three's. Have them separate, take a given amount of time to discuss the question (usually 5 to 15 minutes), and then come back to the group. When everyone is together, present the question again and ask for a response from their smaller groups.

3) Use a role play or skit, but stop it before the conclusion. Ask the group questions concerning what they saw: "What would you do next?" "Should she have said that?" "What values did you see?" "What attitudes were evident?"

4) Create a debate by dividing the group in half and assigning a "pro" side and a "con" side. Subdivide each of these groups into 4 or 5 members. Have the subgroups meet together and create their arguments. Then call on two subgroups to debate with their respective teams behind them for counsel.

5) While planning your presentation or discussion time, write out a few small cards or slips of papers with questions. "Plant" these among participants by asking them to ask this question at the appropriate time. Give them some clue at the top of your note so they know when to ask the question. Tell them to NOT tell others that they have been given the question. Use these planted questions to get the discussion going.

6) Give the participants a handout with basic information, or principles or subject matter. Divide them into groups of two or three and ask them to go over these handouts and put question marks where they have questions, things they don't understand, need more information, or would like examples. Then come to together again and ask, "What questions do you have?" The key is to give handouts that generate questions.

7) Your group enjoys games. So play a game of role reversal. Either after you have presented material, after they have read something, or after the end of a session, tell them: "You are the teacher. I am the students. I have some questions that I would like you to explain." Then play the part of the student and ask questions. Use questions that would clarify issues, compare things, contrast things, challenge something that was said, or ask for examples.

Are there any questions?
If you want to get a discussion going, you need to "set up" for an answer. To drop this question on a group "cold turkey" will usually result in massive silence. When you take into account the many factors in group dynamics, you have a much better chance. If you flop once or twice, do not quit. Failure is still a great teacher.

Index

achieve,drive to, 83
achievements,recognize, 89
advice, 57
antagonist,the, 119
attention getters, 95
attitude,positive, 82
attitudes, 37, 38
believe in them, 79, 82, 83
birth order, 149
brain storming, 66
care,showing you, 80
challenge, 80, 85
challenge to leaders, 2
challenging campers, 79
clothes (see dress), 122
clown,the, 153
communicating, 80
competition,too much, 80
competition,using, 91
complainer, 95
conflict, 94
counseling, 94
counselor, 37
criticism, 30
criticism,destructive, 96
dangers to avoid, 104
demanding the best, 79
Detail, Mr., 71
determination, 17
devotions., 27
diet, 20
director,the, 16
disciple, 17
discipline, 17

discussion, 66
discussion,creating, 167
distractions, 117
dress, 61, 122
emotions, 19
encourage, 82
encouragement, 81, 85, 93
enthusiasm, 80, 117
Esprit De Corps, 93
evaluations, 166
excellence, 79
expectations, 39, 82
failure, 30
failure,overcoming, 86
failure,preventing, 85
failure,using it, 85
fatigue, 29
feedback, 40
Feeler,the, 71
first born, 149
focus, 115
focused,staying, 20, 59, 60, 104
Formula for Success, 115
front,leading from the, 113
games,leading, 115, 129-134
games,planning, 133
gifts, 43
girl\guy relationships, 108
goal setting, 99
goals, 61
goals of youth, 83
grade school age, 139
gripe and grumble, 80
group, 69, 70, 71, 72

Index

grouping campers, 81
groups,making, 78
high school age, 145
Holy Spirit, 24, 27
Holy Spirit working, 21
How To Be A Successful Camp Counselor, 3
How to Lead a Discussion, 167
humility, 23
idea, 58
illness & health, 20
influence, 26
interruptions, 119
junior high age, 141
keeping the fire, 60
language, 62
last born, 153
Leaders
    a servant, 15
    attitudes, 37
    chosen, 13
    communication, 40
    conduct of, 61
    control of emotions, 19
    devoted to group, 81
    example setting, 20
    failure, 30
    focus, 59
    goals, 14
    learning roles, 23
    loneliness of, 29
    mistakes to avoid, 57
    preparation, 22
    respect from, 39
    rewards, 21
    rights of, 29
    risk taking, 58
    self-discipline, 17
    self-starter, 18
    suffering, 14
    time use, 27
    vision,having one, 21
    walking in the Spirit, 26
    wisdom seekers, 22
leadership styles, 47
learn,how people, 157
learning by camper, 85
learning styles, 157
lemon face,the, 118
limitations,know your, 63
listen, 96
LISTEN., 137
love, 37, 38
loyal, 61
manners, 62
money, 19
Moses, 15
MOTIVATION, 77
motivational methods, 77
music, 123
nervous, 114
Nonpartisipation, 117
objectives, 1, 68, 164
Organizer,the, 71
PC rule, 107
personal contact, 107
personality styles, 47
planning, 67
potential, 83

Index

praise,using, 91
prayer, 28, 38, 41, 60, 115
preparation, 113
price of leadership, 28
Pride, 24
pride,group, 81
priorities,setting, 103
problem solving, 57
program, 164, 165
program,changing the, 57
program changes, 58
project, 67, 68
promotion,your, 62
qualification, 25
questions, 66, 68, 72, 166, 167-173
questions to ask, 69
relax!, 114
report,a negative, 57
research, 166
respect, 38, 39, 110
responsibility,, 30
rewards, 103
rewards,using, 90
rights, 29
risk., 58
rules, 79
rules,how to explain, 78
Scripture
    1 Cor. 1:27-28, 14
    1 Cor. 10:13, 19
    1 Cor. 13, 38
    1 Cor. 9:12, 15
    1 Pet. 5:1-7, 36
    1 Sam. 13:14, 13
    1 Tim. 3:2-6, 35
    Acts 6:3, 25, 35
    Col. 1:9, 22
    Eph. 5:18, 25
    Ez. 22:30, 13
    Gal. 2:20, 29
    James 1:19, 137
    James 3, 62
    James 4:6-10, 24
    John 15:16, 13
    Luke 19:17, 18
    Mark 10:43-44, 15
    Matt. 4:1-11, 28
    Matt. 6:33, 14
    Matt. 7:7, 28, 38
    Phil. 1:29-2:11, 15
    Phil. 2:1-17
    , 23
    Prov. 1:7, 22
    Ps. 139:23, 27
    Rom. 8:6-10, 60
second born, 152
self-centered, 94
self-discipline., 17
self-sacrifice, 20
sensitive, 70, 71
sensitivity, 69
servant,being a, 15
sidetracked, 59
song leading, 115, 123
speaking,when, 116
spirit of camp, 25
spiritual gifts, 43
sports, 129
sports,leading, 130

Index

praise,using, 91
prayer, 28, 38, 41, 60, 115
preparation, 113
price of leadership, 28
Pride, 24
pride,group, 81
priorities,setting, 103
problem solving, 57
program, 164, 165
program,changing the, 57
program changes, 58
project, 67, 68
promotion,your, 62
qualification, 25
questions, 66, 68, 72, 166, 167-173
questions to ask, 69
relax!, 114
report,a negative, 57
research, 166
respect, 38, 39, 110
responsibility,, 30
rewards, 103
rewards,using, 90
rights, 29
risk., 58
rules, 79
rules,how to explain, 78

Scripture	page
1 Cor. 1:27-28	14
1 Cor. 10:13	19
1 Cor. 13	38
1 Cor. 9:12	15
1 Pet. 5:1-7	36
1 Sam. 13:14	13
1 Tim. 3:2-6	35
Acts 6:3, 25	35
Col. 1:9	22
Eph. 5:18	25
Ez. 22:30	13
Gal. 2:20	29
James 1:19	137
James 3	62
James 4:6-10	24
John 15:16	13
Luke 19:17	18
Mark 10:43-44	15
Matt. 4:1-11	28
Matt. 6:33,	14
Matt. 7:7	28,38
Phil. 1:29-2:11	15
Phil. 2:1-17	23
Prov. 1:7	22
Ps. 139:23	27
Rom. 8:6-10	60

second born, 152
self-centered, 94
self-discipline., 17
self-sacrifice, 20
sensitive, 70, 71
sensitivity, 69
servant,being a, 15
sidetracked, 59
song leading, 115, 123
speaking,when, 116
spirit of camp, 25
spiritual gifts, 43
sports, 129
sports,leading, 130

NOTES

- Write down page numbers of places of special interest to you.
- Record ideas that come to you when reading.
- Write questions you have, then get answers.
- Find new insights? Add to the book here!

NOTES

- Write down page numbers of places of special interest to you.
- Record ideas that come to you when reading.
- Write questions you have, then get answers.
- Find new insights? Add to the book here!